MICHIGAN

Savor Its Flavors

by Gayle Main

Copyright © 1991 by Gayle Main.

All rights reserved.
No portion of this book may be
reproduced by any means without
permission in writing by the
publisher.

Printed in Michigan.

ISBN 0-9629554-0-X

Published and Distributed by:
Mainly Food
1400 Sebewaing Road
Okemos, MI 48864

*For the farmers of Michigan who produce
these wonderful products for us.*

Photography by Palmini Schroeder Studio, Benton Harbor
Food styling and prop styling by Gayle Main, Okemos
Design and layout by Nancy L. Parker, East Lansing
Editorial assistance by Jane Baker
Research assistance by Carroll Whitehead
Color separations by National Correct Color, Grand Rapids
Printed by The John Henry Company, Lansing

This book was made possible with a grant
from the Michigan Department of Agriculture.

Contents

Michigan Markets	5
Menus	13
Appetizers	23
Soups & Salads	29
Brunch	39
Breads & Sandwiches	45
Main Course	53
Vegetables	71
Desserts	79
Wines & Beverages	89
Index	93

FOREWORD

Today, there's a new focus on cooking and eating: healthy, fast and flavorful. Michigan is a leader in producing food that can be utilized in this style of cooking. Fruits, vegetables and herbs grow here in abundance; meat, fish, poultry and dairy operations dot the state. In fact, Michigan is second in the nation in the number and variety of food products that it produces. In an effort to show consumers how Michigan foods fit today's lifestyle, Michigan commodity organizations, with support from the Michigan Department of Agriculture, joined together to produce this cookbook.

The book offers recipes using only Michigan products as their main ingredients. There is information about the production, nutritional value, and uses for each food product. The commodity groups supplied the recipes and dozens were tested to find ones that were not only nutritious but quick and easy to prepare. Some of the recipes were created for a specific commodity while others are old favorites which were gathered over the years from various sources. Most recipes were altered during testing to meet today's needs and tastes. Full-color photos were taken to bring the taste-tempting appeal of the recipes into focus. Seasonal menus bring all the Michigan products together to make planning for special occasions effortless and enjoyable.

This book showing the abundance of Michigan foods was completely produced by people in Michigan. Every aspect of the cookbook production from the recipe selection and testing to writing and editing to photography to printing to publishing to marketing and distribution was done within the state's borders.

Michigan is a state which is rich in many resources. Michigan's commodity organizations hope you will enjoy this great bounty and savor the flavors of Michigan.

Michigan Markets

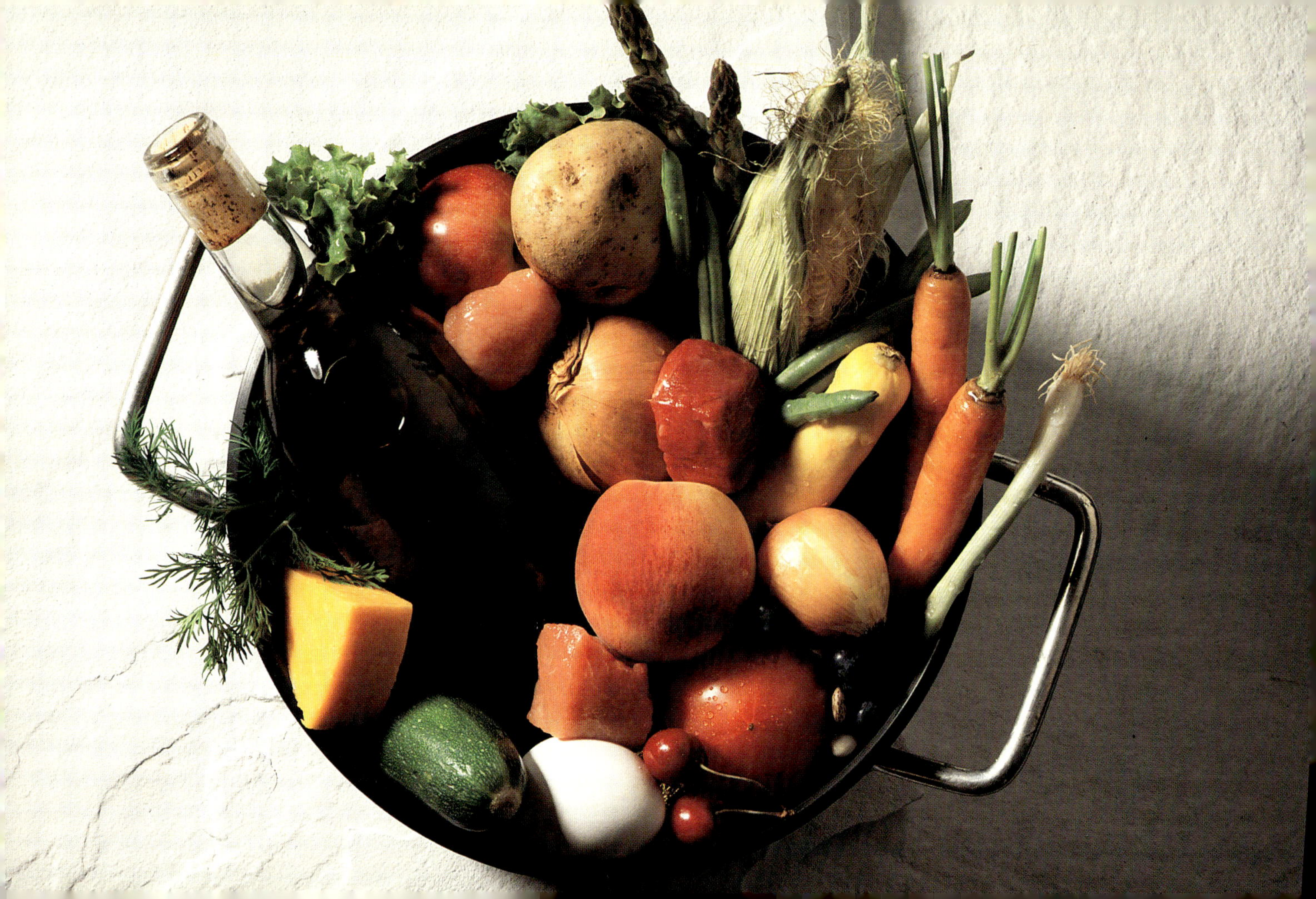

Michigan Markets

With it's rich soil and unique climate, Michigan farmers are able to produce a huge variety and quantity of food products.

The food and agriculture industry is Michigan's second leading industry and employs one out of every 15 Michigan residents. In this chapter, you will find information about Michigan's major food products.

Michigan also produces many other crops including leafy greens, mushrooms, green bell peppers, cucumbers, cauliflower, broccoli, cabbage, tomatoes, pumpkins, squash, cantaloupe, pears, strawberries, wheat, soybeans, and much more.

Put them all together and enjoy a great Michigan meal.

Apples

Michigan ranks second in the nation in apple production, harvesting over one billion pounds each year. The beautiful orchards which dot the state produce a popular fruit which is an excellent source of vitamin A, pectin and fiber. Praised by dentists for reducing tooth decay, apples are also low in sodium, contain only 81 calories and are free of cholesterol. Enjoy the great variety of Michigan apples as a snack, beverage, dessert, salad, or as an ingredient with other foods. Any way you slice them, Michigan apples are a healthy treat.

Asparagus

A symbol of spring in Michigan, the asparagus crop debuts in late April and ends in June. It ranks third in the country. Known for its delicate, delicious flavor, asparagus is low in calories and sodium and high in vitamins and fiber. Shop for fresh asparagus with firm, crisp green stalks and tightly closed, compact tips that are uniform in size for even cooking.. Both the medium and thin stalks are tender. Enjoy asparagus hot with butter or Hollandaise sauce, marinated in a salad, in an omelette or souffle or soup.

Beans

The leader in United States bean production for 100 years, Michigan supplies dry beans throughout the world. An excellent source of low-cost protein, beans are used to make hearty soups, stews, and casseroles. Beans are also high in fiber, calcium, iron and thiamin. Used extensively in classic international dishes, beans can be found in cassoulet, minestroni, and chili con carne.

Beef

Michigan farmers produce a half billion pounds of beef annually. Nutrient-dense beef is an excellent source of protein, iron, zinc, niacin, riboflavin and vitamin B-12. Today's beef is 27% leaner than it was 5 years ago. One 3-ounce portion of lean, trimmed beef has less than 200 calories. This American favorite gives us beef tenderloin, chili, beef stew, the classic hamburger, and grilled steaks just to mention a few.

Blueberries

Since the days when the colonists first landed, native, bush blueberries have been a choice ingredient in traditional American cuisine. Originally, blueberries were just a summer treat, but now they can be frozen and enjoyed all year. The tasty, nutritious fruit has just 42 calories in ½ cup and is a good source of vitamin C. Washed blueberries can be eaten by the handful, sprinkled on cereal or ice cream or yogurt, or used in salads, muffins, pancakes, pies, cakes and sauces. With over 60 million pounds of blueberries harvested annually, Michigan is the nation's "Number 1" producer of blueberries.

Carrots

Get to the root of nutrition with Michigan carrots. This colorful vegetable is an excellent source of vitamin A and dietary fiber and can help fight cancer, ease peptic ulcers and lower blood cholesterol levels. Michigan's rich, black soil is ideal for growing carrots making it one of the largest carrot suppliers in the country. We know carrots best as a crisp raw vegetable snack or a colorful complement to stews. Capitalize on the carrot's versatility and enjoy that nutty-sweet taste and crisp texture in many ways — from soup to dessert!

Celery

America's celery industry was spawned in the areas surrounding Kalamazoo, Michigan. Today, Michigan ranks third in celery production in the nation. A natural health food, celery provides potassium, fiber and vitamin C. Celery is great served raw with a dip or stuffed with cheese. Its flavor enhances a variety of cooked dishes and soups.

Cherries

Michigan cherry trees provide not only a delectable edible, but a feast for the eyes when cherry blossoms bloom in the spring. You know them best as the key ingredient in cherry pie and cherry cheesecake, but cherries are more than dessert. This bright, flavorful and wholesome fruit is also tasty when used in main courses, side dishes, salads, and breads. Not only do cherries have great taste and versatility, they are nutritious. Cherries are high in vitamin A and potassium; they are low in calories, fat and sodium. Michigan is the leading producer of red tart cherries in the United States, producing 70% to 75% of the crop.

Corn

Also called maize, corn is classified as sweet corn, field corn or popcorn. Sweet corn may be white or yellow and should be refrigerated to maintain freshness and sweetness. Field corn is used largely to feed livestock but is also used to make cornmeal, oil, syrup and breakfast cereals. Popcorn, an excellent source of fiber, is one of America's favorite snacks. A good source of carbohydrates and vitamin C, corn can be steamed, boiled, microwaved, or grilled. Michigan produces over 100 million ears of sweet corn each year making it the sixth largest producer in the nation.

Dairy Products

Milk and milk products have played a vital role in Michigan's history since Sieur Antoine de la Mothe Cadillac established farms in the city of Detroit during the early 1700's. Since those early days, the industry has continued to serve the nutritional needs of a growing state with a wide variety of wholesome and refreshing products including cheese, ice cream, yogurt, butter and milk. Dairy farming contributes over $15 billion a year to Michigan's economy. Dairy products are very popular because of their taste, variety and versatility. They are also nutritious supplying 76% of the calcium in the food supply.

Goat Cheese (chevre)

Always considered a luxury in France, goat cheese is now made in Michigan and known as Michigan chevre. The goat cheeses being produced in our state today have opened up a whole new world of taste. They are fresh, tangy, zesty and widely available. Lower in calories and easier to digest than many other cheeses, goat cheese is a good source of protein, calcium, and vitamins. Delicious in salads, entrees, omelets and desserts, goat cheese will add variety to your Michigan menus.

Grapes & Wine

Grapes grown in Michigan are used to make jams, jellies, preserves, grape juice, wine or sold as a fresh-market commodity. Michigan ranks fifth in grape production and sixth in wine production in the nation. The Lake Michigan shore region has proven to be ideal for grape and wine production and Michigan wines have won numerous awards. The state's seventeen wineries produce almost 50 million bottles of wine each year. Enjoy a variety of Michigan wines including red, white, blush, fruit, sparkling champagne and sparkling fruit juices.

Herbs

With their sweet smells, fresh flavors, and beautiful leaves and blossoms, herbs are the delight of cooks and gardeners.

Culinary herbs give foods exceptional flavoring without adding salt. The leaves and flowers of herbs add distinction to a meal when used as garnishes or as an edible part of a salad or other dish. Herbal teas, vinegars, butters, jams, jellies, and condiments are available at the dozens of beautiful herb farms and gardens located in Michigan.

Honey

With nearly 100,000 bee colonies in Michigan, the state ranks in the top ten honey producers in the nation. The variety of clovers and wild flowers that grow abundantly in Michigan make the flavor of the honey exceptional. Used to sweeten beverages, baked goods, sauces, and entrees, honey has been an American favorite since colonists imported honey bees from Europe in the 1600's. Honey bees also pollinate about one-third of our food-producing crops.

Lamb

The juicy tenderness and delicate flavor of today's lamb make it an ideal choice for a gourmet meal, family supper, or grilling outdoors. It is low in calories and high in nutrients. A standard, three-ounce portion contains just 176 calories and is an excellent source of protein, iron, zinc and B-vitamins. Lamb is a traditional favorite in the spring but is available year round for kabobs, chops, and roasted leg of lamb just to name a few. Michigan produces about 125,000 lambs each year.

Maple Syrup

The first farm crop harvested each year, maple sap flows as early as February when warm days are followed by freezing nights. It takes 40 gallons of sap to produce one gallon of pure maple syrup. Average maple syrup production in Michigan is 90,000 gallons each year positioning Michigan in fifth place nationally among syrup producers. Maple syrup is 100% pure with no additives, coloring, or preservatives. It is a marvelous ingredient for baked goods and candy, a delicious addition to meats and baked beans and a wonderful topping for pancakes, fruit, and ice cream.

Onions

For flavor, texture and versatility, onions have few peers and have played a starring role in almost every cuisine on earth. Onions have been found to lower blood pressure, reduce cholesterol levels in the blood, and help stop dangerous blood clots. Being a good source of fiber and vitamin C, onions also reduce the chances of contracting cancer. Michigan produces over 220 million pounds of onions each year including dry onions, leeks, scallions, shallots and chives. There is no need to cry over your onions. Peel under running water or slice all but the root part of the onion which causes the irritating fumes to be released. Cooking onions brings out their sweet flavor.

PEACHES

With over a million peach trees, Michigan is the sixth largest producer in the nation. Reach for a peach and enjoy a fruit which is high in vitamin A and potassium and low in calories. Don't rely on the "blush" complexion as an indicator of ripeness. The better test is how it feels and smells. Ripe peaches should be firm, aromatic and tender along the line running the length of the fruit. Enjoy peaches in a salad, with cheese, as an accompaniment to an entree or as a delicious snack.

PLUMS

Plums are the most widely-distributed of all native fruits in America. Michigan is the nation's second largest producer of this deciduous tree's fruit. Michigan plum growers specialize in Italian plums which are large and purple. They are excellent fresh, canned or frozen and can be used in salads, pies, dumplings, preserves, jams, jellies, or as a snack. Besides being plum good, they are nutritious. Purple plums are high in calcium, vitamins A and C, and fiber while low in fat and calories.

PORK

It's a fact. Today's pork is leaner and lower in fat and calories than ever before. This change is the result of new breeding and feeding practices as well as closer trimming of retail cuts. An average 3-ounce serving of cooked, trimmed pork has only 198 calories and is high in protein, thiamin, niacin, zinc and iron. Lean cuts such as loin, tenderloin and fresh ham are available boneless for convenience. Today's pork does not need to be overcooked — 160 degrees Fahrenheit is optimum for flavor and safety. Michigan farmers raise two million hogs annually which places Michigan 11th in pork production and 5th in pork processing in the country.

POTATOES

Americans love potatoes and eat more of them than all other vegetables combined. They have been a staple for the poor and humble as well as a delicacy for the gourmet. We love them baked, boiled, mashed, broiled, fried or microwaved for breakfast, lunch, dinner and snacks. The versatile potato is quick and easy to prepare and nutritious. A good source of carbohydrates, iron and vitamin C, potatoes are also low in sodium, fat-free and contain only 90 calories each when baked. Potatoes are the largest vegetable crop in Michigan. Farmers from one end of the state to the other produce over a billion pounds of potatoes each year.

POULTRY & EGGS

The variety of ways to prepare poultry and eggs seems to be endless.

The traditional turkey which was once seen only on Thanksgiving is now a staple item at the grocery store. We use it on our deli sandwiches, in casseroles, grilled and microwaved. It is also used to make salami, bologna and hot dogs since it is so low in fat. Michigan farmers raise over four million turkeys each year and almost six million chickens.

Most American's eat chicken two or three times each week. It's easy on the budget as well as the waistline and is welcome in soup kitchens, on picnics, and in the finest restaurants. It is a good source of protein and vitamin B and is low in fat.

Each of us eat about 270 eggs each year in the form of bread, cakes, souffles, omelets, custards, quiche, sauces, meringues, and more. A great source of protein, vitamin A, vitamin D and iron, health-conscious consumers use two egg whites instead of one egg yolk in recipes to lower the cholesterol level. Six million hens produce 1½ billion eggs each year in Michigan.

Sugar Beets

Just about everyone likes sugar. For most of us, sugar and foods sweetened with sugar conjure up life's happiest moments —birthdays, holidays, and celebrations of all kinds. Michigan ranks fifth in the production of sugar beets in the United States. Sugar is a carbohydrate that occurs naturally in every fruit and vegetable. Sugar occurs in greatest quantities in sugarcane and sugar beets from which it is separated for commercial use. In its refined form, sugar plays important roles in baking bread, preserving fruit, freezing ice cream and preparing foods of all kinds, from pancakes to spaghetti sauce.

Veal

Naturally lean, delicious and easy to prepare, veal fits today's healthful, uncomplicated way of cooking and eating. And veal's versatility can't be beat. Depending upon the cut and cooking method, veal can be elegant enough for the most special occasion or just right for a budget-wise weekday meal. Classic French and Italian recipes such as veal Parmesan, Piccata, Marsala and Osso Buco are delicious and easy to prepare. Veal is also great on the grill, in stir-fry dishes or simply broiled or sauteed. Nutrient dense veal is high is protein, zinc, niacin and vitamin B-12. It is also very low in fat and contains just 166 calories per 3-ounce serving.

Whitefish

Truly a gift from the sea, the Great Lakes of Michigan produce between eight and nine million pounds of whitefish annually. The delicate, almost sweet, snow-white meat is a healthy and delicious dining choice. Whitefish is high in protein and low in fat with only 150 calories in a 3-ounce serving. A bonus from the whitefish are their eggs. The roe from whitefish, which spawn in the shoal waters of the lakes, is marketed as golden caviar. A true delicacy, whitefish caviar has a mild flavor and is not oily. Serve it with Michigan wine for a special treat.

Menus

Winter Menus

New Year's Eve Dinner

Superior Whitefish Pate*

Great Lakes Green Salad*

Blueberry Sauced
Veal Medallions*

Rice Pilaf

Hot Buttery Green Beans

Cherries Jubilee*

Michigan Champagne

Ski Slope Supper

Hot Florentine Dip with Whole
Wheat Crackers*

Party Chili
with Assorted Toppings*

Cheese Bread Bowls*

Crisp Green Salad

Snowcap Blueberry
Ice Cream Pie*

Peach Wine Warmer*

Anniversary Celebration Dinner

Fresh Onion Soup*

Poached Beef Tenderloin*

Herbed New Potatoes*

Honey Glazed Carrots*

Brussels Sprouts

Poppyseed Rolls

Apple Dumplings
with Dried Cherries*

Michigan Red Wine

*Recipes included in book.

Right: Blueberry Sauced Veal Medallions and Green Beans

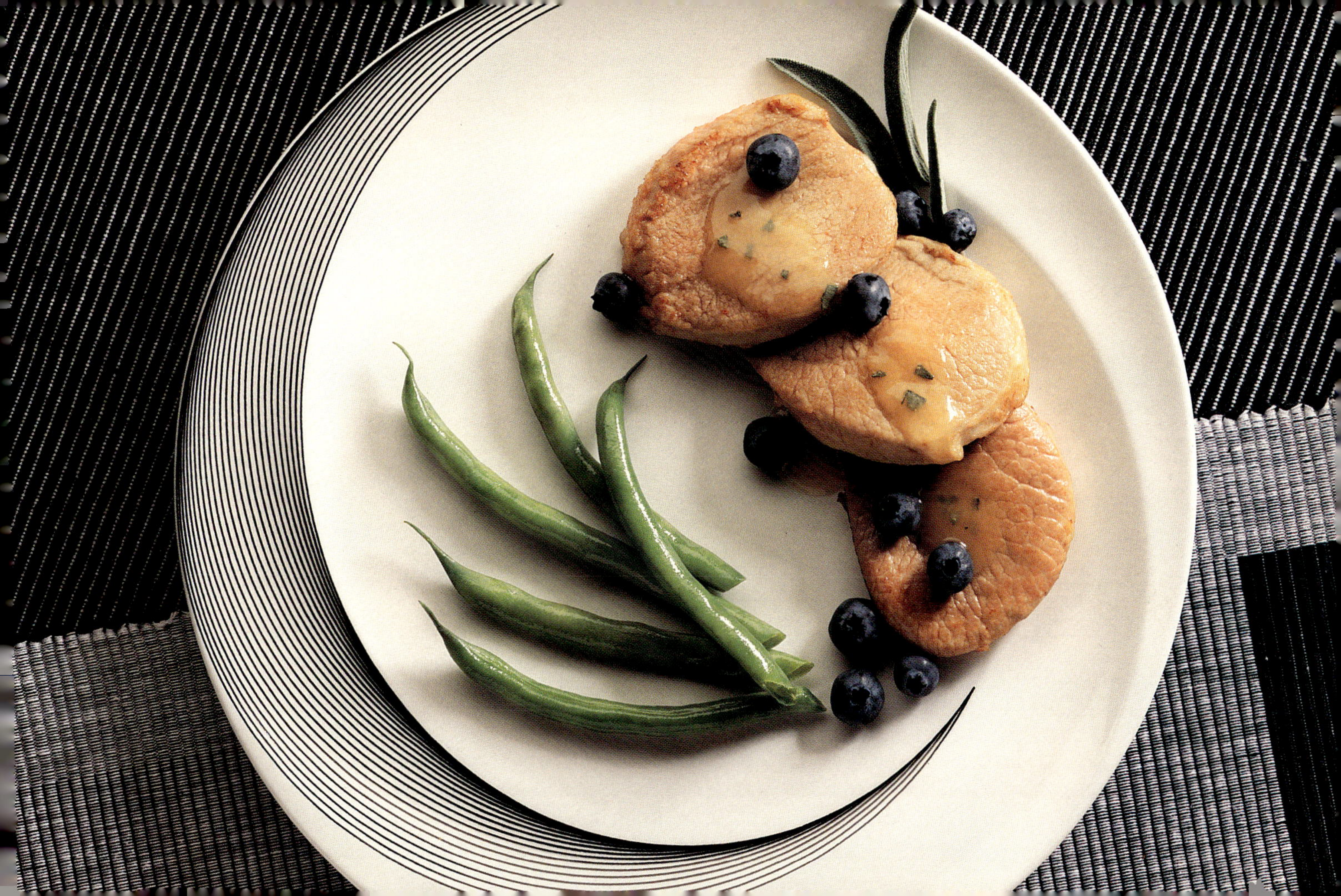

Spring Menus

Sunday Dinner In May

Baked Brie with Strawberries*

Cucumber Soup*

Roast Lamb with Mint Sauce*

Carrots and
Asparagus Spears

Cloverleaf Rolls with Butter

Chocolate Cherry Cheesecake*

Michigan White Wine

Herb Garden Luncheon

Cheddar Chive Crisps*

Cream of Asparagus Soup*

Flowering Garden Salad*

Hot Chicken and Celery Salad*

Pasta and Pesto*

Herb Biscuits and Butter*

Maple Fresh Fruit Cup*

Minted Ice Tea

Mother's Day Brunch

Festive Oven Omelet*

Strawberry French Toast
with Maple Syrup*

Marinated Asparagus*

Carrot-Apple Salad*

Medley of Fresh Fruits

Peach Brunch Cake*

Raspberry Cream Cheese Torte*

Sparkling Cherry Punch*

*Recipes included in book.

Right: Roast Lamb with Mint Sauce and Asparagus and Carrots

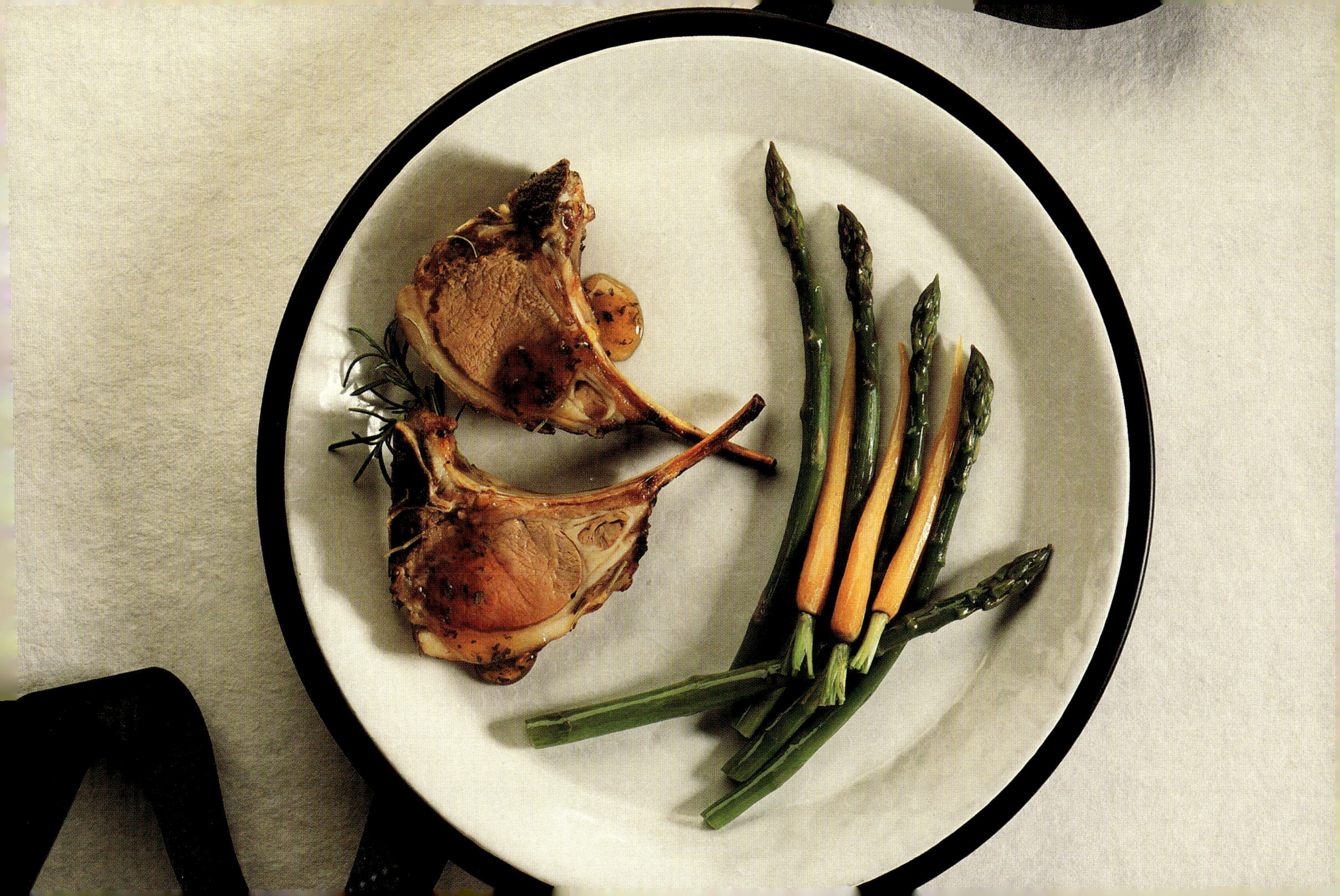

Summer Menus

Backyard Barbecue

*Apple Stuffed Celery**
*Maple Barbecued Spareribs**
*Grilled Stuffed Potatoes**
*Hot Peppery Corn-on-the-Cob**
*Picnic Bean Salad**
*Grilled Cheddar Loaf**
Strawberry Shortcake
Fresh Lemonade

Sunset Dinner by the Lake

Assorted Meats with Melon
*Grilled Chicken with Peach Salsa**
Fresh Garden Pea Pods
*Colorful Cabbage Salad**
Corn Bread Muffins
*Cheesecake Squares**
*White Wine Cooler**

Fisherman's Catch

Assorted Cheese and Crackers
Green and Purple Grapes
*Fish Fillets with Garden Vegetables**
*Potato Wedges**
*Blueberry Muffins**
*Orchard Streusel Cake**
Michigan White Wine

*Recipes included in book.

Right: Maple Barbecued Spareribs, Hot Peppery Corn-on-the-Cob and Picnic Bean Salad

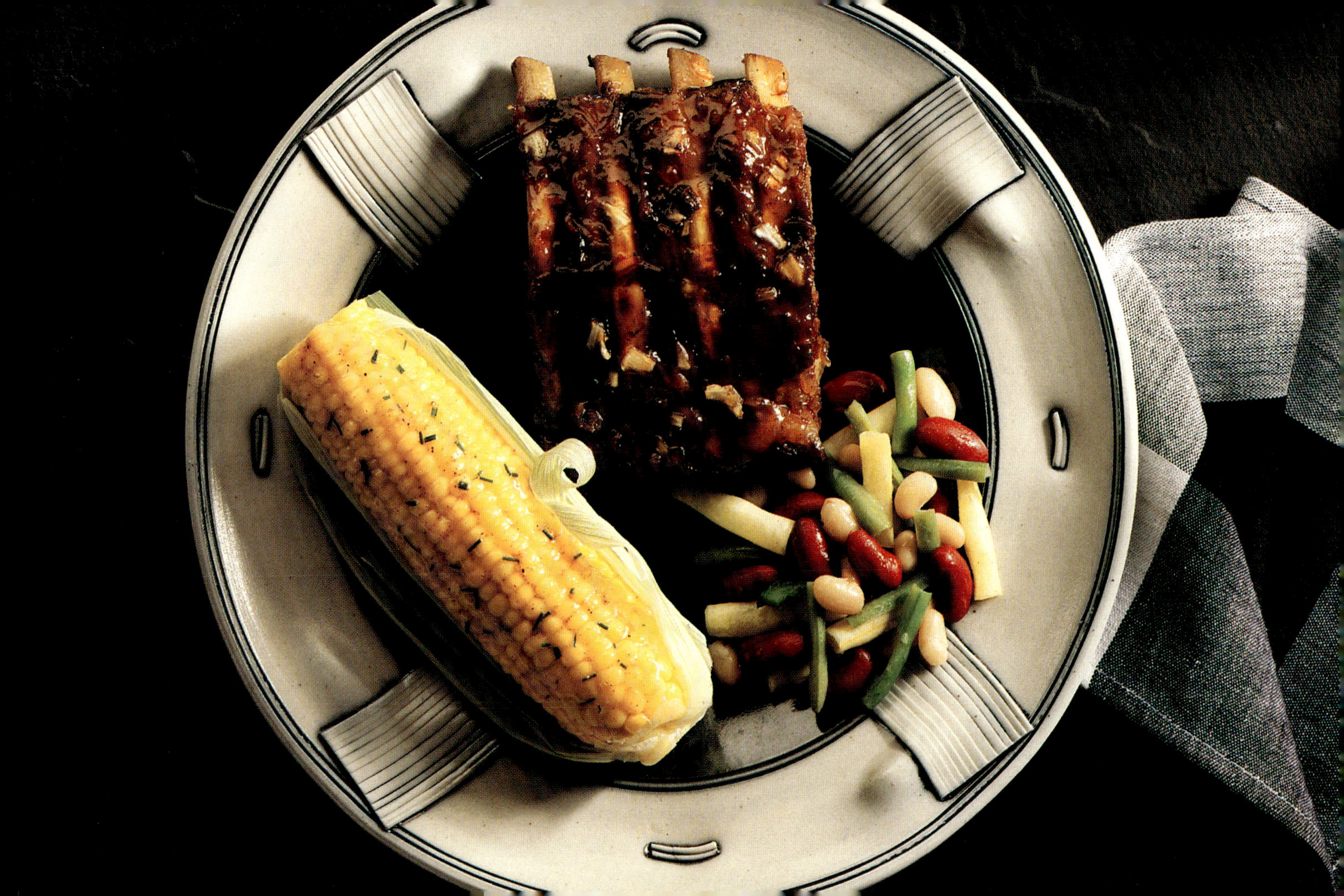

Fall Menus

Autumn Tailgate Picnic

Victory Pass Pate*

Apple Dipper*

Tailgate Roll-ups*

Michigan Senate Bean Soup*

Asparagus Pasta Salad*

Chocolate Brownies

Spiced Apple Cider*

Fireside Feast

Fresh Vegetables with Green Onion Dip*

Spinach Salad with Hot Bacon Dressing

Pork Medallions with Rosemary and Mushrooms*

Brown and Wild Rice

Baked Acorn Squash

Traverse Bay Cherry-Nut Cake*

Michigan White Wine

Holiday Dinner

Cheddar Pinecone with Assorted Crackers*

Pumpkin Soup*

Turkey with Cherry Wine Sauce*

Steamed Broccoli Spears

Baked Celery*

Spiced Plum Bread*

Maple Pecan Squares with Whipped Cream*

Sparkling Grape Juice

*Recipes included in book.

Right: Turkey with Cherry Wine Sauce and Broccoli Spears

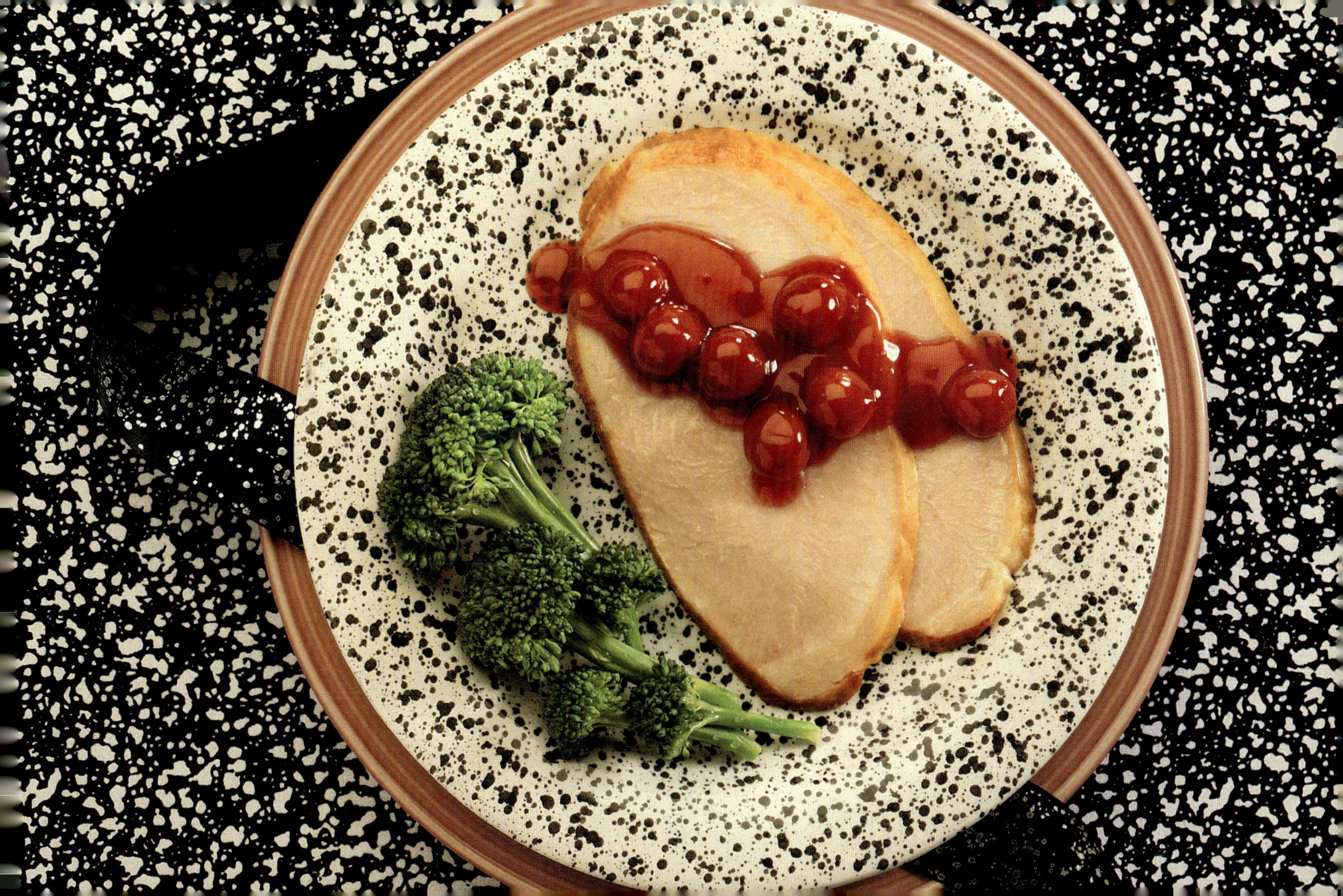

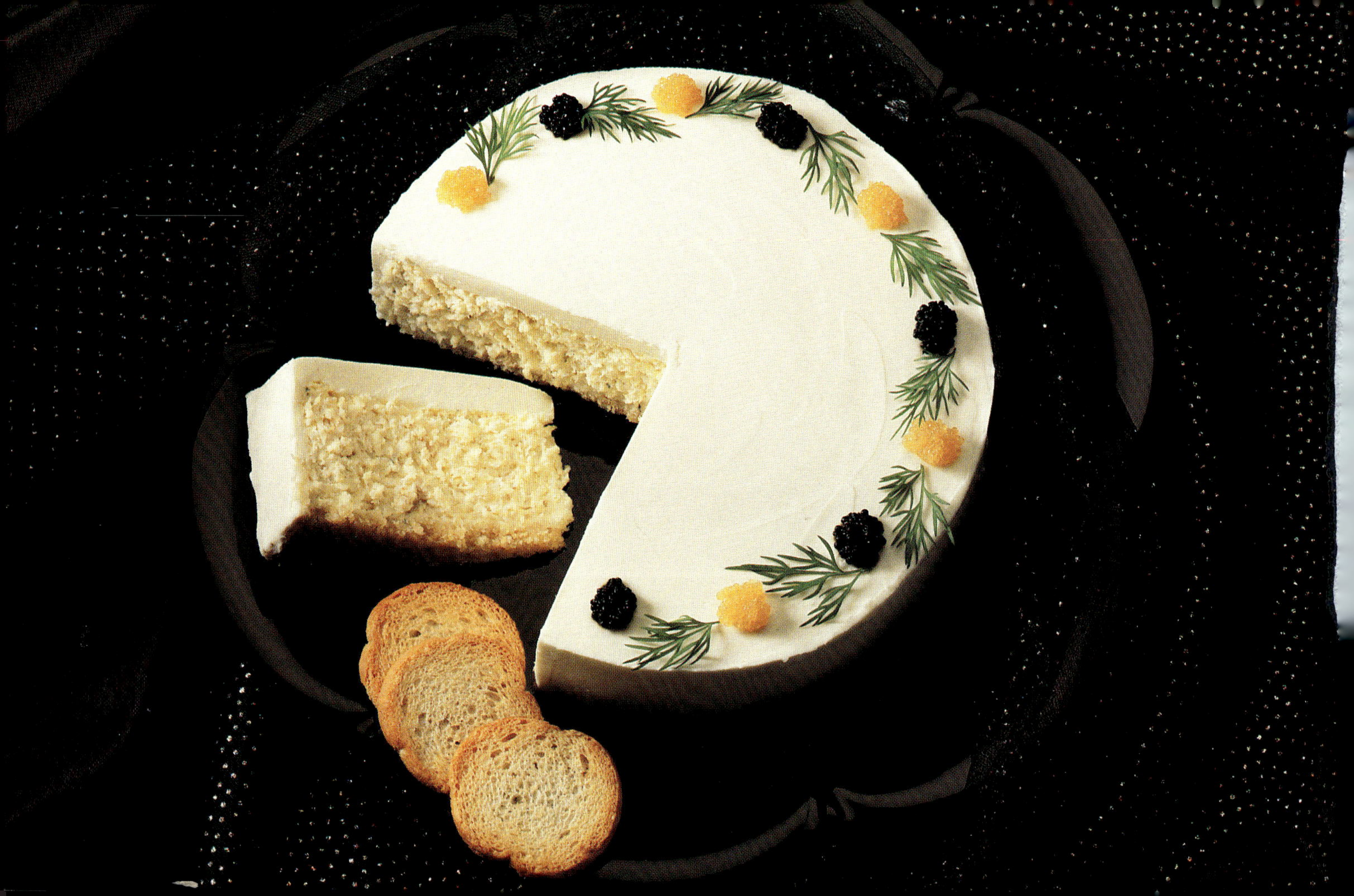

Appetizers

Left: Superior Whitefish Pate

Superior Whitefish Pate

1 tablespoon butter
1 cup bread crumbs
3/4 cup grated Parmesan cheese
2 teaspoons minced dillweed, divided
4 1/2 tablespoons melted butter, divided
2 packages (8 ounces each) cream cheese, softened
2 eggs
1/3 cup milk
1/3 cup shredded Monterey Jack cheese
1/4 teaspoon white pepper
1/4 teaspoon Old Bay seasoning
Dash cayenne pepper
1/2 teaspoon salt
5 ounces smoked whitefish, finely chopped
1/2 ounce black whitefish caviar for garnish, optional
1/2 ounce golden whitefish caviar for garnish, optional
Fresh dillweed for garnish, optional

Prepare an 8-inch springform pan by spreading 1 tablespoon butter on inside bottom and sides. In a small bowl, combine bread crumbs, Parmesan cheese, 1 teaspoon dillweed and 3 tablespoons melted butter. To form crust, press crumb mixture onto bottom of springform pan.

In medium mixing bowl, beat cream cheese with electric mixer until smooth. Add eggs, remaining 1½ tablespoons melted butter, milk, Monterey Jack cheese, white pepper, Old Bay seasoning, cayenne pepper and salt; mix well. Stir in whitefish. Pour batter into springform pan. Bake in a 325-degree oven for 1¼ hours, or until almost solid.

Let cool completely. Garnish with caviar and dillweed.

Makes 16 appetizer servings.

Baked Brie with Strawberries

1 round loaf (1 pound) whole-grain bread, unsliced
1 pound wheel Brie cheese with rind, 6-inches in diameter
1 pint fresh strawberries, hulled

Slice off the top ½-inch of bread; discard or save for another use.. Remove enough bread from the center of the loaf to set cheese inside. Insert cheese into bread and wrap with foil. Bake in a 350-degree oven 30 minutes, or untill cheese begins to melt. Halve strawberries and arrange on top of cheese in a circular pattern. Slice into wedges to serve. Serve warm.
Makes 16 to 20 servings.

Green Onion Dip

2 green onions
1 package (8 ounces) cream cheese, chilled
Assorted fresh vegetables and crackers

Rinse green onions and pat dry with paper towel. Cut off the root end of green onions and discard.
Cut remainder of onions into 1-inch pieces. With the motor of food processor running continuously, drop the onion pieces into the food processor bowl through the food chute. Process until finely chopped.
Cut cream cheese into 8 equal parts. With the motor running continuously, drop pieces of cream cheese into the bowl one at at time. Process 1 minute, or until the dip is smooth and light green. Serve with fresh vegetables or crackers.
Makes about 1 cup of dip.

Apple Dipper

1 package (8 ounces) cream cheese,
    softened
1 cup shredded Cheddar cheese
2 tablespoons apple juice
    or apple cider
2 red apples
2 teaspoons chopped chives
Dash salt
1 green apple
1 golden yellow apple
2 teaspoons ascorbic acid powder
    (such as Fruit Fresh)
3 tablespoons water

In a medium bowl, combine cream cheese, Cheddar cheese and apple juice. Mix until smooth. Peel, core and grate 1 red apple. Stir into cheese mixture. Add chives and salt; mix well. Refrigerate several hours to blend flavors.

To serve, mix ascorbic acid powder and water in a small bowl. Core and slice remaining red apple, green apple and golden yellow apple. Immediately toss sliced apples in ascorbic acid mixture to prevent browning. Arrange apple slices, alternating colors, around cheese mixture. Serve immediately.

Makes 8 to 10 appetizer servings.

Apple Stuffed Celery

1 medium red apple,
    cored and finely chopped
1/4 cup finely chopped walnuts
1 package (3 ounces) cream cheese,
    softened
2 teaspoons lemon juice, optional
6 celery stalks, rinsed
    and cut into 3-inch lengths

In a small mixing bowl, combine apple, walnuts, cream cheese and lemon juice; mix well. Use to stuff celery.

Makes about 6 appetizer servings.

Hot Florentine Dip

1 package (10 ounces) frozen chopped spinach, thawed
1 package (8 ounces) cream cheese, softened
2 tablespoons milk
2 tablespoons finely chopped onion
3/4 teaspoon garlic salt
1/2 teaspoon black pepper
1 can (6 3/4 ounces) chunk ham, drained
1 cup sour cream
3/4 cup chopped pecans (about 3 ounces)
Assorted crackers

Cook spinach according to package directions; drain well. Squeeze excess moisture out with paper towels. In a medium mixing bowl, combine cream cheese, milk, onion, garlic salt and pepper; mix well. Stir in ham and spinach. Fold in sour cream and pecans. Pour mixture into a 2-quart baking dish. Bake in a preheated 350-degree oven 15 minutes, or until bubbly. Serve warm with crackers.

Makes 12 servings.

Cheddar Pine Cone

2 cups (8 ounces) shredded Cheddar cheese
2 packages (3 ounces each) cream cheese, softened
1/4 cup chopped pimiento-stuffed olives
1 1/2 tablespoons mayonnaise
1/4 teaspoon Worcestershire sauce
1 tablespoon grated onion
Dash garlic salt and celery salt
1/4 cup sliced almonds
Assorted crackers and fresh vegetables

In a large mixing bowl, combine Cheddar cheese, cream cheese, olives, mayonnaise, Worcestershire sauce and onion. Mix until smooth. Season with garlic salt and celery salt. Shape cheese mixture into a 6-inch long oval. Arrange almonds over surface to resemble a pine cone, pressing ends of almonds gently into cheese mixture to get them to adhere. Serve with crackers and vegetables.

Makes about 3 cups.

VICTORY PASS PATE

1 pound chicken livers
1/2 cup white wine
3/4 cup chicken broth
1/4 cup finely chopped onion
2 to 3 sprigs fresh parsley
1/4 teaspoon ground ginger
1 tablespoon soy sauce
1/2 cup butter or margarine, softened
1/2 teaspoon salt
1/4 teaspoon dry mustard
1 tablespoon brandy, optional
Pimiento strips for garnish
Assorted crackers

In a medium saucepan, combine chicken livers, wine, chicken broth, onion, parsley, ginger and soy sauce. Cook over medium heat until chicken livers are tender. Remove from heat and let cool in liquid. Drain, reserving ¼ cup cooking liquid. Puree chicken livers in a food processor or electric blender. Add butter, salt, mustard and brandy; process until smooth and well blended. Add reserved cooking liquid, if desired, to make a softer mixture. Refrigerate 24 hours to blend flavors.

To serve, place pate on a platter and form into the shape of a football. Garnish with pimiento strips to form the ties of the football; surround with crackers.

Makes 1½ to 2 cups.

CHEDDAR CHIVE CRISPS

1/2 cup butter
1 cup all-purpose flour
1/2 teaspoon salt
1/2 teaspoon baking powder
2 cups (8 ounces) finely shredded sharp Cheddar cheese
2 cups crisp rice cereal
1/4 cup snipped fresh chives

In a medium mixing bowl, beat butter until light and fluffy. On a piece of waxed paper, combine flour, salt and baking powder. Gradually add to butter and mix well. Stir in cheese and cereal. Shape dough into a log 11 inches long and 2 inches in diameter. Roll log in chives. Wrap in waxed paper and let chill several hours until firm. Cut chilled dough into ¼-inch slices; place on an ungreased baking sheet. Bake in 350-degree oven for 12 to 15 minutes, or until golden brown. Serve immediately.

Makes 3 dozen.

Soups & Salads

Pumpkin Soup

6 small pumpkins (1 pound each)
1 medium pumpkin (about 2 pounds)
2 tablespoons butter or margarine
1 cup chopped onion
1 clove garlic, peeled and chopped
1/2 cup all-purpose flour
6 cups chicken broth
1/2 teaspoon salt
1/2 teaspoon dried thyme leaves, crushed
5 whole black peppercorns
1/2 cup heavy cream
2 strips bacon, cooked crisp and crumbled

With a sharp knife, cut tops off small pumpkins. Scoop out and discard seeds and stringy pulp to make containers for the soup. Set aside pumpkin bowls.

Cut top off medium pumpkin. Scrape out and discard seeds and stringy pulp. Place pumpkin in microwave oven on a paper towel. Microwave on HIGH (100% power) 5 to 10 minutes, or until pumpkin is tender. Remove outer skin; cut pumpkin into ½-inch cubes. Set aside about 3 cups of cubes.

In a large saucepan, melt butter. Add onion, garlic and flour; mix well. Cook over medium heat until mixture is bubbly. Remove from heat; stir in chicken broth, mixing until smooth.

Return to heat and cook over high heat until mixture is bubbly and slightly thickened. Add cooked pumpkin cubes, salt, thyme and peppercorns. Reduce heat; cover saucepan and simmer 30 minutes.

Pour soup mixture into a large bowl. Puree soup mixture, 2 cups at a time, in a food processor or electric blender. Return pureed soup mixture to saucepan. Cook over medium heat until hot, but not boiling. Stir in cream; mix well.

Meanwhile, warm pumpkin bowls in a preheated 350-degree oven 20 minutes.

Divide soup evenly among pumpkin bowls. Garnish with bacon.

Makes 6 servings.

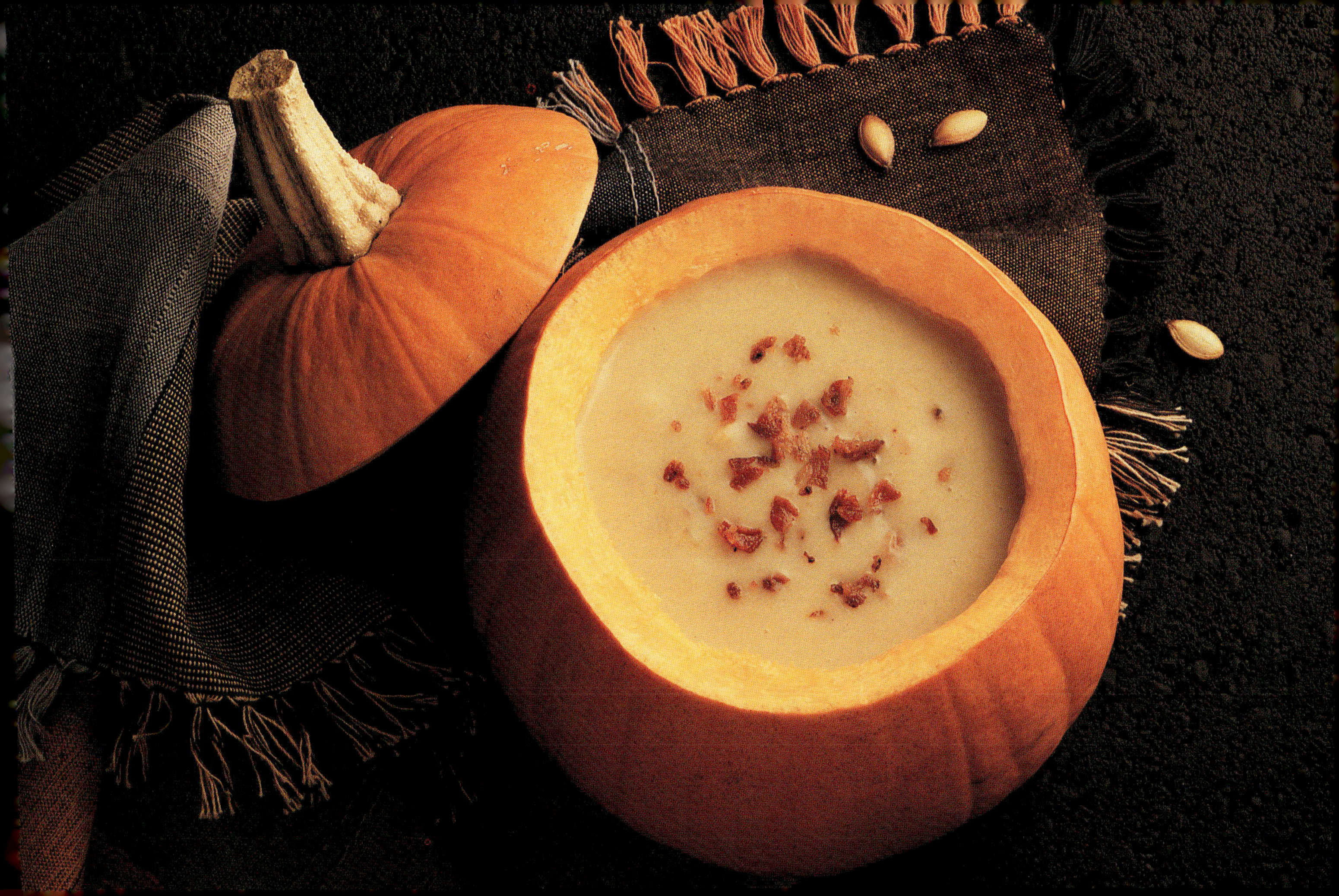

Fresh Onion Soup

1/4 cup butter or margarine
2 tablespoons vegetable oil
7 cups thinly sliced onions
　(about 2 pounds)
1 teaspoon salt
2 quarts beef broth
3 tablespoons all-purpose flour
1/8 teaspoon ground black pepper
6 to 8 French bread slices,
　1-inch thick, toasted
2 cups grated Swiss cheese

Melt butter and oil in a large saucepan. Add onions and salt; cook over medium-low heat 30 minutes, stirring frequently, until onions are golden brown. Sprinkle with flour and cook 2 to 3 minutes, stirring constantly. Add beef broth and stir to blend. Cover; simmer 30 minutes.

To serve, ladle soup in oven-proof bowls; place a slice of toasted bread on top of each serving. Sprinkle cheese evenly over bread. Broil, 3 to 4 inches from heat, until cheese melts and begins to brown.

Makes 6 to 8 servings.

Michigan Senate Bean Soup

1 pound dry navy beans
10 cups cold water
1 1/2 pound meaty ham bone
1 1/2 teaspoons salt
1/2 teaspoon ground black pepper
1 bay leaf
1 large onion, chopped

Wash and sort navy beans. In large saucepan, combine beans and 8 cups cold water. Bring to a boil; simmer 2 minutes. Remove from heat; cover and let stand 1 hour. Do not drain. Add ham bone, salt, pepper and bay leaf. Cover and heat to boiling. Reduce heat; simmer 3 hours, or until beans are tender. Add 2 more cups water and chopped onion. Simmer 30 minutes. Remove ham bone and cut ham off the bone. Set meat aside and discard ham bone. With a potato masher, gently mash beans, if desired. Add ham to soup and season with salt and pepper.

Makes 6 servings.

Cream of Asparagus Soup

1 small onion, chopped
3 tablespoons butter or margarine
1/2 cup water
1 cup peeled, diced potato
1 1/2 cups chicken broth
1/2 teaspoon celery salt
1 pound asparagus,
　cut into 1-inch pieces
1 cup light cream or milk
Salt and pepper
Minced parsley, chives,
　or asparagus tips

　In a small saucepan, bring onion, butter, water, potato and broth to a boil. Simmer until potato is tender. Add celery salt and asparagus. Bring to a boil; simmer 10 minutes. Pour soup mixture into a large bowl; let cool. Puree soup mixture, 2 cups at at time, in a food processor or electric blender. Pour back into saucepan; add cream. Heat thoroughly. Season with salt and pepper to taste. Garnish with parsley, chives or asparagus tips.
　Makes 4 servings.

　Variations: Substitute broccoli, carrots, cauliflower or mushrooms for asparagus.

Cucumber Soup

1 tablespoon unsalted butter
1 cucumber, peeled and cubed
2 cans (14 ounces each) beef broth

　In a medium saucepan, melt butter. Add cucumber; saute 2 minutes, or until tender crisp. Add beef broth; simmer 15 minutes. Serve immediately.
　Makes 4 servings.

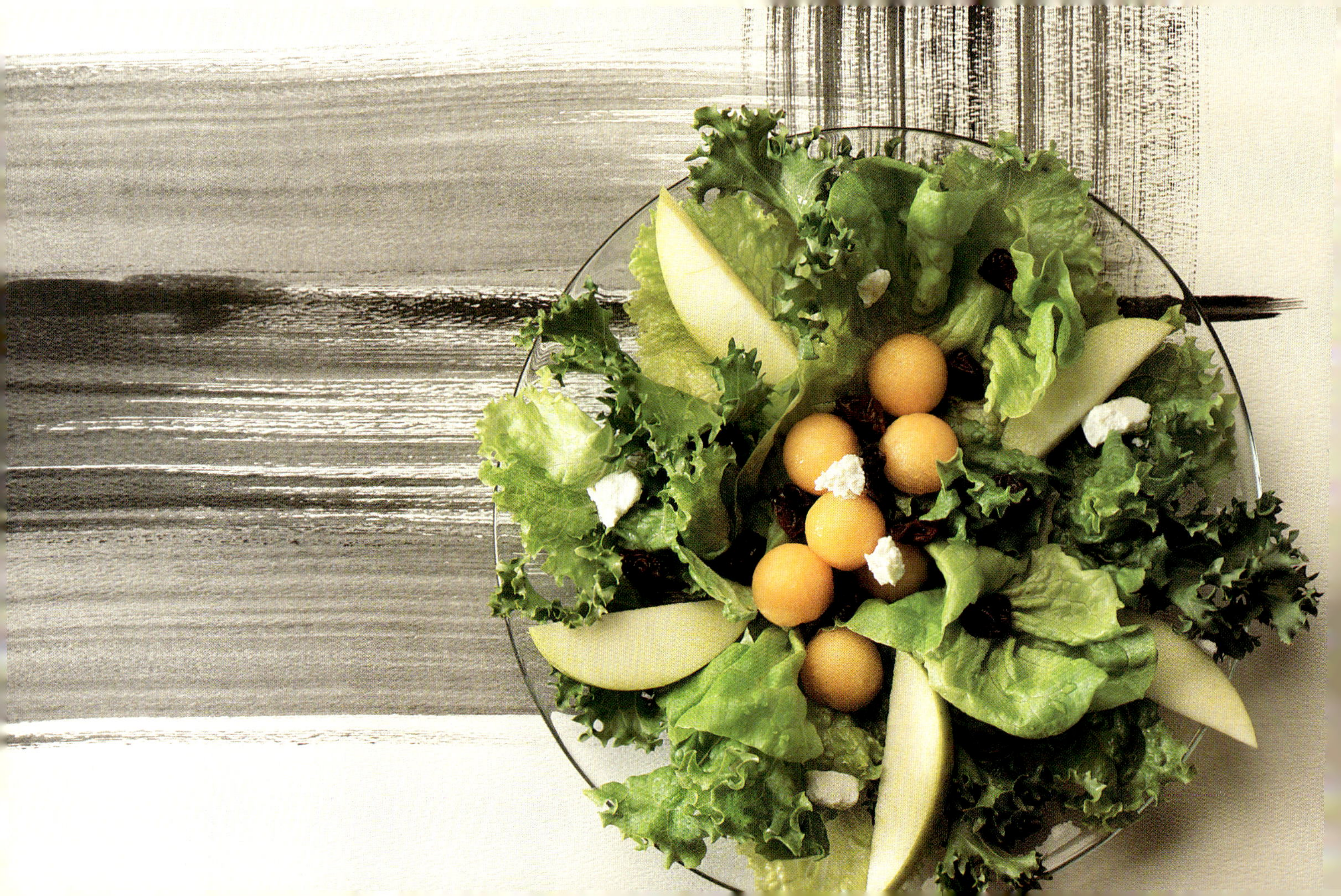

Great Lakes Green Salad

4 to 5 cups torn salad greens such as escarole, endive, leaf, Boston or your favorite.
1/2 cup dried cherries
1 apple, cored and sliced
1 cup melon balls
1/4 cup chevre (goat cheese), crumbled
Dried Cherry Vinaigrette
  (recipe follows)

  Rinse salad greens, drain and pat dry.
  In a large serving bowl, toss together salad greens, cherries, apple slices, melon balls and goat cheese. Serve with Dried Cherry Vinaigrette.
  Makes 4 to 6 servings.

Dried Cherry Vinaigrette
1/4 cup cherry vinegar (instructions follow)
1/4 cup vegetable oil
1/4 teaspoon salt
1/4 teaspoon freshly ground black pepper

  In a small bowl, combine vinegar, oil, salt and pepper. Mix well.
  Makes about ½ cup.

  To make cherry vinegar: In a 1-quart container, combine 1 cup dried cherries and 2 cups white wine vinegar. Cover and let steep 2 days at room temperature.
  In a medium pan, bring vinegar mixture just to boiling. Strain through cheesecloth; discard cherries. Let vinegar cool. Store in a tightly sealed container.
  Makes 2 cups vinegar.

Asparagus Pasta Salad

1 cup small shell pasta, uncooked
1 pound fresh asparagus,
  cut into 1 1/2-inch pieces
1/2 cup thinly sliced carrots
1/2 cup chopped onion
1/4 cup chopped red bell pepper
1 teaspoon dried oregano
1/2 teaspoon celery seeds
1/2 cup Italian salad dressing

  Cook pasta according to package directions. Rinse, drain and cool.
  Steam asparagus, carrots and onions until crisp-tender. Drain well.
  In a large salad bowl or other container, combine cooked pasta, steamed vegetables, red pepper, oregano and celery seeds. Add salad dressing; mix well. Refrigerate 6 to 8 hours, or overnight, to blend flavors. Toss salad before serving.
  Makes 6 to 8 servings.

Left: Great Lakes Green Salad

Pasta and Pesto

2 cups fresh basil leaves,
   rinsed and well drained
1/2 cups fresh parsley
2 to 3 cloves garlic, peeled
   and lightly crushed
1/2 cup pine nuts, optional
1 cup olive oil
1 cup freshly grated Parmesan cheese
Salt to taste
2 tablespoons hot water
2 pounds hot, cooked pasta

Place basil, parsley, garlic and pine nuts in electric blender or food processor; blend until finely chopped. With motor running on high speed, slowly add oil and blend until smooth. Stir in cheese. Season with salt.

Before serving add hot water to pesto sauce, which allows sauce to cover pasta more easily. Do not add water until you are ready to use the sauce. Combine sauce and pasta; mix well. Serve immediately.

Makes 2 cups pesto; 8 servings of pasta.

Note: Pesto sauce can be stored in the refrigerator for up to 2 weeks by topping with a thin layer of olive oil. Pesto sauce also is good as a topping for meats, fish and tomato salads.

Flowering Garden Salad

1/3 cup raspberry vinegar
2 teaspoon Dijon mustard
1 clove garlic, peeled
    and finely chopped
1/4 teaspoon dried thyme, crushed
1/4 teaspoon salt
1/8 teaspoon ground black pepper
1 cup vegetable oil
6 cups torn assorted lettuce leaves
    such as red leaf, Bibb and Boston
1/2 cup whole pecans
1 can (5 ounces) sliced water
    chestnuts, drained and rinsed
1 to 2 cups edible flowers, such as
    violets, nasturtiums, pansies
    or rose petals (see note)

    In a small container, combine vinegar, mustard, garlic, thyme, salt, pepper and oil. Stir vigorously to mix.
    Rinse lettuce, drain and pat dry.
    Divide lettuce, pecans and water chestnuts among 4 salad plates. Garnish each serving with flowers. Drizzle dressing over each portion.
    Makes 4 servings.

Note: Make sure flowers used in this recipe are edible. Rinse well and drain before using.

Picnic Bean Salad

1 can (16 ounces) Great Northern beans,
    drained
1 pound fresh green beans,
    cut in 1-inch pieces and blanched
1 pound fresh yellow wax beans,
    cut in 1-inch pieces and blanched
1 can (16 ounces) dark red kidney beans,
    drained
3/4 cup chopped green pepper
1/2 cup chopped onion
1/2 cup vegetable oil
1/2 cup cider vinegar
3/4 cup granulated sugar
1 teaspoon salt
1/2 teaspoon black pepper

    In a large serving bowl, combine Great Northern beans, green beans, wax beans, kidney beans, green pepper and onion. In a small bowl, combine oil, vinegar, sugar, salt and pepper. Pour over bean mixture and toss. Refrigerate, covered, until ready to serve.
    Makes 10 servings.

Colorful Cabbage Salad

2 cups shredded green cabbage
1 cup shredded red cabbbage
2 tablespoons sliced green onions
1/2 cup sour cream
2 tablespoons granulated sugar
1/2 teaspoon salt

In a large serving bowl, combine green and red cabbage, onion, sour cream, sugar and salt; mix well. Cover and refrigerate to blend flavors before serving.

Makes 6 servings.

Carrot-Apple Salad

2 cups shredded carrots
1 1/2 cups diced, unpeeled apples
1/2 cup raisins
1/4 cup chopped walnuts
1/2 cup mayonnaise or salad dressing
1 tablespoon lemon juice
1 tablespoon honey
Lettuce leaves

In a serving bowl, combine carrots, apples, raisins and walnuts. In a small bowl, combine mayonnaise, lemon juice and honey; mix well. Pour dressing over carrot mixture; toss until coated. Cover and chill. Serve on lettuce leaves.

Makes 6 servings.

Brunch

Three Onion Tart

1 cup all-purpose flour
2 tablespoons whole wheat flour
1/2 teaspoon salt, divided
1/4 cup butter or margarine, well chilled
2 to 3 tablespoons water
2 teaspoon olive oil
1 cup coarsely chopped onion
3/4 cup sliced leeks, white part only
1/4 cup sliced green onions
1 cup milk
2 eggs
2 teaspoons cornstarch
1/4 teaspoon freshly ground black pepper
1/4 teaspoon of cayenne pepper
2 ounces Gruyere cheese, cubed

In a medium mixing bowl, combine all-purpose flour, whole wheat flour and ¼ teaspoon salt. Cut in butter with a pastry blender or fork until mixture forms coarse crumbs. Stir in water, 1 tablespoon at a time, just until dough forms. Gather dough into a ball; place in a pastic bag and chill 30 minutes.

Place chilled ball of dough between 2 large sheets of waxed paper and roll into an 11-inch circle. Press dough into the bottom and up the sides of a 9-inch fluted tart pan, letting dough extend ¼-inch above edges of pan. Prick bottom and sides of dough with a fork. Place tart pan on a baking sheet. Bake in a preheated 375-degree oven 10 minutes, or until crust is golden brown. Let cool slightly on a wire rack.

Heat olive oil in a medium skillet over medium heat. Add onion, leeks and green onions. Saute 5 to 7 minutes, or until tender. Remove from heat; set aside.

In a medium bowl, combine milk, eggs, cornstarch, remaining ¼ teaspoon salt, black pepper and cayenne; mix well. Set aside.

To assemble, put onion mixture in the bottom of partially cooled, baked crust. Add cheese. Pour egg mixture over onions and cheese. Bake in a preheated 375-degree oven 25 to 30 minutes, or until filling is set and golden brown.

Makes 6 servings.

Right: Three Onion Tart

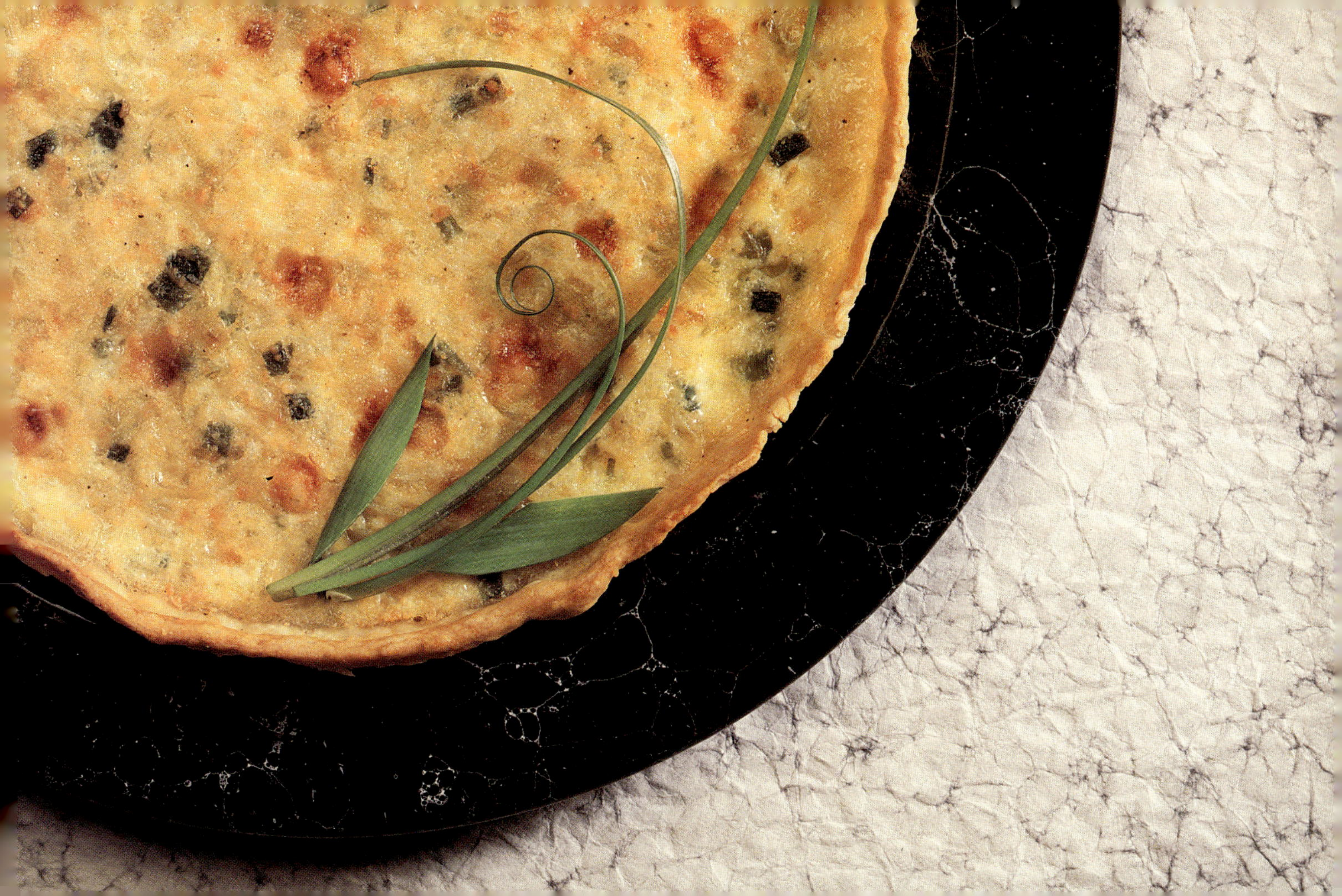

Festive Oven Omelet

1/4 cup butter or margarine
16 eggs
1 cup sour cream
1 cup milk
1/4 teaspoon salt
1/4 teaspoon dried basil leaves, crushed
2 cups (8 ounces) shredded Cheddar or American processed cheese
1 can (4 ounces) mushroom stems and pieces, drained
4 green onions, thinly sliced
1 jar (2 ounces) diced pimiento, drained

Melt butter in a 13x9x2-inch baking pan in a 325-degree oven. Tilt pan to coat with melted butter. Set aside.

In a large mixing bowl, combine eggs, sour cream, milk, salt and basil; mix well. Stir in cheese, mushrooms, green onions and pimiento. Pour into prepared pan.

Bake in a preheated 325-degree oven 40 to 45 minutes, or until omelet is set, but still moist. Serve immediately.

Makes 12 servings.

Buttered Plum Waffles

1/4 cup butter or margarine
1/2 cup granulated sugar
2 teaspoons cornstarch
1/8 teaspoon freshly grated nutmeg
4 cups quartered, pitted purple plums
1/2 teaspoon vanilla extract
Juice and grated rind of 1 small orange
6 waffles, cooked

In a large skillet, melt butter over medium heat. Remove skillet from heat. Stir in sugar, cornstarch and nutmeg; mix well. Stir in plums, turning to coat with sugar mixture. Cook over medium heat, stirring occasionally, 3 to 5 minutes, or until plums release enough juice to make a sauce.

Remove from heat. Gently stir in vanilla, orange juice and grated orange rind. Cook over high heat, stirring constantly, 2 to 3 minutes, or until sauce boils and mixture thickens. Serve hot plums and sauce over warm waffles.

Makes 6 servings.

Strawberry French Toast with Maple Syrup

4 tablespoon butter or margarine
3 eggs, beaten
1 cup milk
2 tablespoons granulated sugar
1 teaspoon vanilla extract
12 slices French bread,
   cut in 1-inch thick slices
1 quart strawberries, hulled and
   quartered
Sweetened whipped cream
Warm maple syrup

In a 375-degree oven, melt butter in a 15x9x1-inch jelly roll pan. Tilt pan so butter covers it evenly. In medium mixing bowl, whisk together eggs, milk, sugar and vanilla. Place each piece of bread in egg mixture on both sides. Place bread in one layer in buttered pan. Bake in a preheated 375-degree oven 15 minutes. Turn bread and bake another 10 minutes. To serve, place toast on serving plate. Top with strawberries and a swirl of whipped cream. Top with maple syrup.

Makes 6 servings.

Broccoli Quiche

3 eggs, slightly beaten
1/3 cup milk
1 package (10 ounces) chopped
   broccoli, thawed and drained
1 can (3 ounces) French fried
   onion rings, divided
1 cup shredded Cheddar cheese,
   divided
1/2 teaspoon salt
1/8 teaspoon freshy ground pepper
1 baked 9-inch pie crust

In medium mixing bowl, beat eggs and milk together. Stir in broccoli, ½ can onion rings, ½ cup cheese, salt and pepper. Pour into pie shell. Microwave on MEDIUM (50% power) 8 to 15 minutes, or until almost set, rotating ¼ turn every 4 minutes. Sprinkle remaining onion rings and cheese over top. Microwave on MEDIUM 1 to 3 minutes, or until cheese melts. Let stand 5 minutes before serving.

Makes 6 servings.

Peach Brunch Cake

1/2 cup butter or margarine, softened
1/4 cup plus 3 tablespoons granulated sugar, divided
1 teaspoon vanilla extract
1 egg
1 cup sifted all-purpose flour
1/2 teaspoon baking powder
1/4 teaspoon salt
1 can (28 ounces) sliced peaches, well drained
1/2 teaspoon ground cinnamon

In a small mixing bowl with an electric mixer, beat butter and ¼ cup sugar until light and fluffy. Add vanilla and egg; beat well.

Mix flour, baking powder and salt together on a piece of waxed paper. Add to butter mixture; blend well. Spread batter over bottom and 1 inch up the sides of a greased 9-inch springform pan.

Arrange peach slices in a spoke fashion over batter. Combine remaining 3 tablespoons sugar and cinnamon; sprinkle over peaches.

Bake in a preheated 350-degree oven 30 to 35 minutes, or until edges are golden brown. Let cool in pan on wire rack 10 minutes. Remove sides of pan. Serve warm.

Makes 8 servings.

Breads & Sandwiches

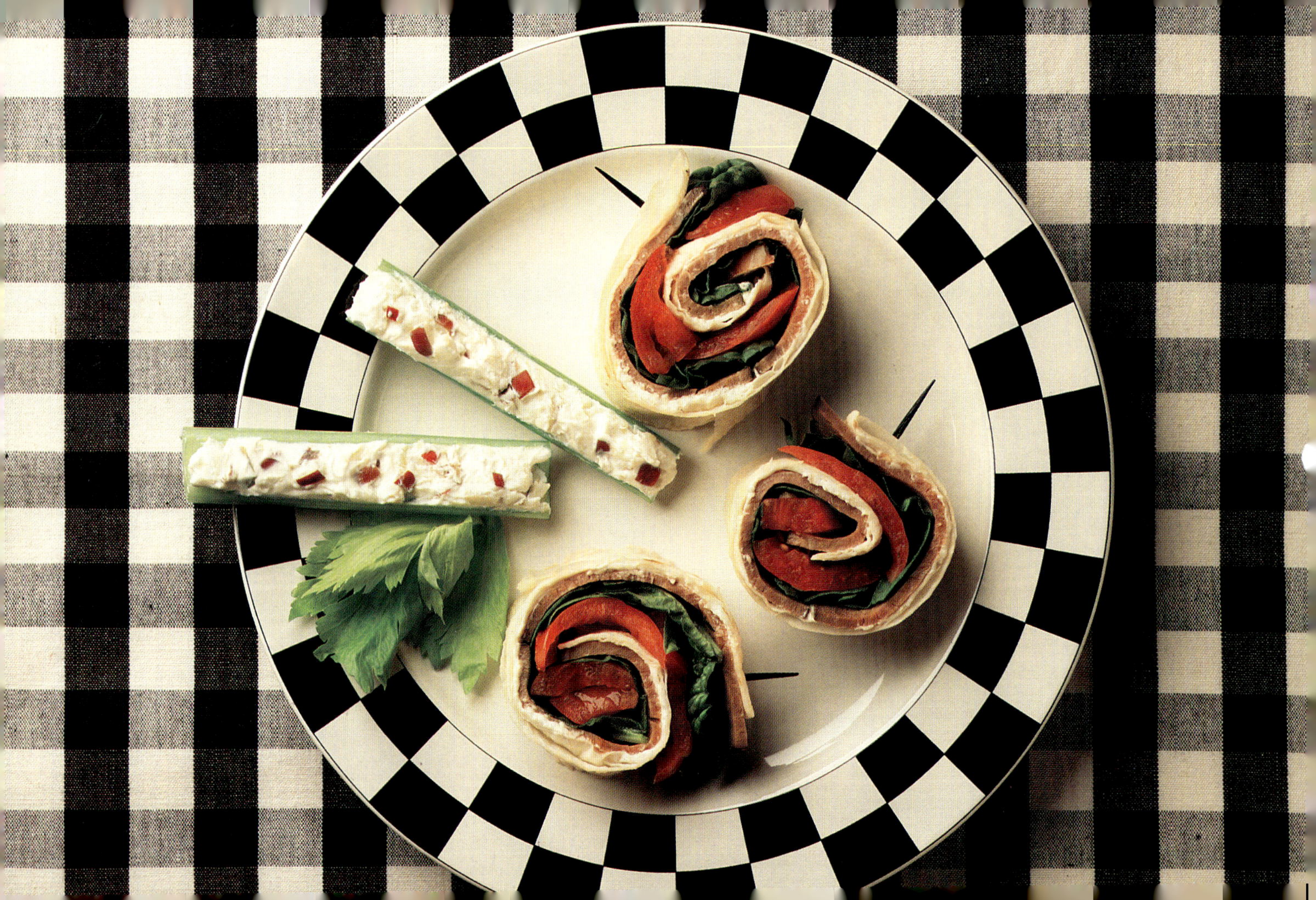

Tailgate Roll-ups

1 package (8 ounces) cream cheese, softened
2 tablespoons milk
1 tablespoon prepared horseradish
1/4 teaspoon ground black pepper
4 (8-inch) flour tortillas
1/2 pound thinly sliced roast beef
2 medium tomatoes, cored and sliced very thin
1/2 pound fresh spinach, rinsed and well drained with stems removed

In a small bowl, beat cream cheese until light and fluffy. Stir in milk, horseradish and pepper; mix well. If necessary, add more milk so mixture will spread easily.

Lightly moisten both sides of each tortilla with water. Lay tortillas on a flat surface and spread each with a generous portion of cheese mixture. Layer beef, tomatoes and spinach evenly over cheese mixture.

Roll up each tortilla, jelly-roll fashion. Wrap each roll in a damp paper towel, then in plastic wrap. Refrigerate up to 4 hours. To serve, cut each roll into 2- to 3-inch pieces.

Makes 4 servings.

Left: Tailgate Roll-ups and Apple Stuffed Celery

Zucchini Pockets

1 teaspoon butter or margarine
1 cup sliced zucchini
1/2 cup sliced yellow summer squash
1/2 cup sliced fresh mushrooms
1 cup chopped tomato
1/2 teaspoon dried basil leaves, crushed
1/4 teaspoon garlic powder
2 tablespoons grated Parmesan cheese
4 small pocket breads

Melt butter in a large skillet. Add zucchini, yellow summer squash and mushrooms; cook until tender. Drain off excess liquid. Stir in tomato, basil, garlic powder and Parmesan cheese. Split open one end of each pocket bread. Divide zucchini mixture into four equal portions and spoon into pocket breads.

Makes 4 servings.

Note: Vegetable filling also may be served as a side dish.

Omelet in a Bread Round

1/4 cup finely chopped
   pimiento-stuffed green olives
6 tablespoons butter or margarine,
   divided
1 round loaf (16 ounces) bread,
   not sliced
1/2 cup chopped onions
1/4 pound mushrooms, finely chopped
1/4 pound cooked ham, chopped
1 large, cooked potato,
   peeled and chopped
1/2 cup sliced pimiento-stuffed olives
12 eggs, well beaten

In a small container, combine chopped olives and 2 tablespoons butter; mix well. With a sharp knife, cut bread horizontally in half. Scoop out soft center of bottom half of bread, leaving 1-inch wide shell. Spread cut surfaces, including cut surface of top half, with olive mixture. Reassemble loaf, wrap in foil and keep warm in a 300-degree oven while preparing omelet.

Melt 2 tablespoons butter in a 10-inch skillet. Add onions and mushrooms; cook until tender. Remove onion mixture from pan. Melt remaining 2 tablespoons butter in skillet used to cook vegetables, then pour in half the beaten eggs. Cook over medium heat until eggs begin to set. Cover with onion mixture, ham, potato and sliced olives. Add remaining eggs. Cook, vigorously shaking pan to allow uncooked egg mixture to flow underneath. To finish cooking, place omelet under broiler for 1 to 2 minutes, or until brown.

Remove bread from oven; lift omelet out of skillet and into scooped out portion of bread. Cover with top half of bread; cut into wedges and serve immediately.

Makes 6 servings.

Note: To serve at a picnic, wrap omelet-filled bread in 4 layers of heavy-duty aluminum foil to keep warm up to 3 hours.

To prepare omelet ahead of time, wrap omelet-filled bread in aluminum foil and chill. Reheat in a 400-degree oven 25 to 30 minutes.

Herb Biscuits

2 cups all-purpose flour
2 teaspoons baking powder
1/2 teaspoon baking soda
1 teaspoon salt
5 tablespoons unsalted butter, chilled
2 tablespoons finely chopped fresh parsley
2 tablespoons finely chopped fresh dill or chives
1 cup buttermilk

In a large mixing bowl, sift together flour, baking powder, baking soda and salt. Cut in butter with pastry blender or fork until mixture resembles coarse crumbs. Stir in parsley and dill. Add buttermilk and stir just until flour is moistened.

Turn dough onto a lightly floured surface. Knead gently just until dough comes together, sprinkling lightly with additional flour to keep it from sticking to the surface. Roll out dough to ½-inch thickness. Cut into 2-inch rounds or heart shapes and arrange 1-inch apart on ungreased baking sheets. Combine scraps and re-roll; use to make as many biscuits as possible.

Bake in a preheated 450-degree oven 10 minutes, or until tops are golden. Makes 15 biscuits.

Herb Butter

1/2 cup butter, softened
2 tablespoon chopped fresh dill (or 1/2 teaspoon dried dillweed)
1 tablespoon chopped fresh parsley (or 1 teaspoon dried parsley flakes)
1 tablespoon chopped fresh chives (or 1 teaspoon dried chives)
1 1/2 teaspoons lemon juice

In a small mixing bowl with an electric mixer, beat butter, dill, parsley, chives and lemon juice until light and fluffy. Cover and let stand 3 hours to blend flavors. Herb Butter will keep up to 3 days when made with fresh herbs and several weeks when made with dried herbs. Use on baked or boiled potatoes, grilled fish, vegetables or hot, crusty French bread.

Makes ½ cup.

Grilled Cheddar Loaf

1 loaf (16 ounces) French bread, not sliced
1 cup (4 ounces) shredded Cheddar cheese
1/4 cup mayonnaise
3 tablespoons chopped green onions
1/2 teaspoon chili powder
2 tablespoons sliced ripe olives

Cut bread in half lengthwise. Set aside.

In a small bowl, combine cheese, mayonnaise, onions and chili powder. Mix well. Spread each half of bread with cheese mixture. Arrange olive slices over cheese mixture. Wrap each bread half loosely in foil.

Place on grill over hot coals and heat 10 to 15 minutes, or until cheese is melted. (Or bake in a preheated 350-degree oven 10 to 15 minutes)

Makes 12 servings.

Cheese Bread Bowls

1 package active dry yeast
2 cups all-purpose flour, divided
1 jar (5 ounces) Old English cheese spread
1/2 cup water
1/4 cup solid vegetable shortening
2 tablespoons granulated sugar
3/4 teaspoon salt
1 egg, beaten
1 egg white

In a medium mixing bowl, combine yeast and 1 cup flour; set aside.

In a small saucepan, combine cheese spread, water, shortening, sugar and salt. Cook over medium heat, stirring constantly, until cheese spread is melted and mixture is 105 to 115 degrees. Add cheese mixture and beaten egg to yeast mixture. With an electric mixer on low speed, beat 30 seconds, scraping sides of bowl. Beat 3 minutes on high speed. Stir in remaining 1 cup flour.

Turn dough onto a lightly floured surface. Knead dough 1 to 2 minutes. Divide dough into 8 equal-sized balls. On a lightly floured surface, roll each ball into a 6-inch circle. Shape dough circles over the bottom of 8 well-greased, 10-ounce custard cups. Place cups, bottom side up, on 2 greased baking sheets. The dough should not touch the baking sheet.

Bake in a preheated 375-degree oven 10 minutes. Remove from oven and carefully remove bread bowls from custard cups with a knife. Place bread bowls right side up on baking sheets.

Combine egg white and 1 tablespoon water; beat until frothy. Brush egg white mixture over outside and inside of bread bowls; do not brush outside bottom. Return to preheated 375-degree oven and bake 5 minutes, or until bowls are brown on the outside edges. Fill with Party Chili (Recipe on Page 56) and serve immediately.

Makes 8 bread bowls.

Note: This recipe is also good for serving salads and stews.

Spiced Plum Bread

1 can (16 ounces) purple plums
2/3 cup granulated sugar
1/2 cup honey
1 egg
1 teaspoon vanilla extract
2 cups all-purpose flour
1 teaspoon baking soda
1/4 teaspoon ground cloves
1/8 teaspoon ground cinnamon
1 cup chopped walnuts

Drain and pit plums; chop them into small pieces. Set aside.

In a large mixing bowl with an electric mixer, combine sugar, honey, egg and vanilla. Mix until well blended. On a sheet of waxed paper, combine flour, baking soda, cloves and cinnamon; add to sugar mixture. Stir in chopped plums and walnuts. Do not overmix. Pour batter into a lightly greased 9x5x3-inch baking pan.

Bake in a preheated 350-degree oven 50 to 60 minutes, or until wooden pick come out clean. If top becomes too brown, cover loosely with aluminum foil to prevent overbrowning. Remove bread from pan and let cool on wire rack.

Makes 1 loaf.

Blueberry Muffins

1/4 cup butter or margarine
1/2 cup granulated sugar
1 egg
1/2 cup milk
1-1/2 cups all-purpose flour
2 teaspoons baking powder
1/4 teaspoon salt
3/4 to 1 cup fresh or frozen blueberries, rinsed (or thawed) and drained

In a large mixing bowl with an electric mixer, beat butter and sugar until light and fluffy. Add egg and milk; mix well. Stir in flour, baking powder and salt until just moistened; batter will be lumpy. Fold in blueberries. Spoon batter into greased muffin pans, filling each two-thirds full.

Bake in a preheated 350-degree oven 25 minutes, or until golden brown. Remove from pans immediately and serve warm.

Makes 12 muffins.

Main Course

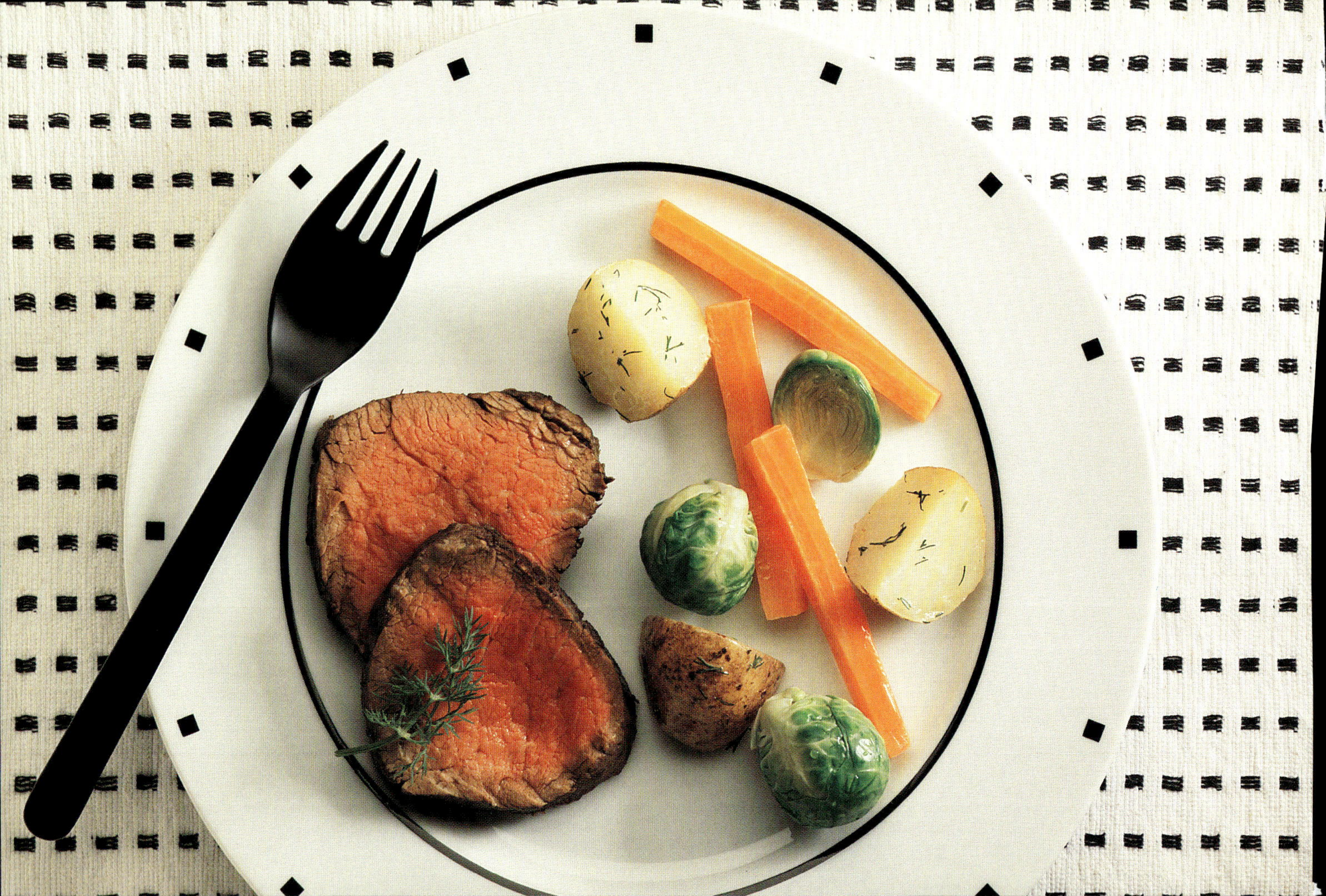

Poached Beef Tenderloin

1 (2 pound) beef tenderloin roast
1 tablespoon vegetable oil
4 cups water
1 can (10 1/2 ounces) condensed beef broth
1 cup dry red wine
2 cloves garlic, peeled and finely chopped
1 teaspoon dried marjoram leaves
4 whole black peppercorns
3 whole cloves

Tie roast with a heavy string at 2-inch intervals. In a Dutch oven, brown roast in oil over medium-high heat until all sides are browned. Pour off drippings.

Add water, beef broth, wine, garlic, marjoram, peppercorns and cloves. Bring to a boil; reduce heat to medium-low, cover and simmer 10 minutes per pound. (Internal temperature of roast should register 130 degrees on a meat thermometer.) Do not overcook roast.

Remove roast to serving platter. Cover tightly with plastic wrap or aluminum foil. Allow roast to stand 10 minutes before carving. (During this standing time the internal temperature of the roast will rise to about 140 degrees for rare.) Remove string and carve roast into thin slices.

Makes 8 servings.

Note: Center slices of this roast will be rare; end cuts will be medium rare. Cooking a beef tenderloin roast to well done by this method is not recommended.

Left: Poached Beef Tenderloin, Herbed New Potatoes, Honey Glazed Carrots and Brussels Sprouts

Pepper Beef Kabobs

1 pound boneless beef top sirloin steak, cut into 1-inch cubes
1 cup soy sauce
1 piece (1-inch long) chopped, fresh ginger root
1/3 cup red wine vinegar
1 clove garlic, minced
1/4 cup dark brown sugar
3 tablespoons chopped onion
1 teaspoon coarsely ground pepper

Place beef cubes in a plastic bag. Combine soy sauce, ginger root, vinegar, garlic, brown sugar and onion; mix well. Pour over beef cubes. Close bag and marinate 30 minutes.

Remove beef cubes and sprinkle with pepper, pressing it gently into the surface of the meat. Thread beef on 4 (9-inch) metal skewers. Place kabobs on rack in broiler pan. Broil, 3 to 4 inches from heat, 10 to 13 minutes to doneness desired, turning occasionally.

Makes 4 servings.

Party Chili

1 pound lean ground beef
1 medium onion, chopped
1 medium green pepper,
    seeded and chopped
2 cloves garlic, finely chopped
3 cups water
1 can (16 ounces) kidney beans,
    drained
1 can (12 ounces) tomato paste
1 can (16 ounces) tomatoes,
    undrained and chopped
1/4 to 1/2 cup diced ripe olives
1 jalapeno pepper, finely chopped
2 tablespoons chili powder
1 1/2 tablespoons brown sugar
1/2 teaspoon salt
1/2 teaspoon garlic salt
1/4 teaspoon ground cumin
1/4 teaspoon ground black pepper

Cheese Bread Bowls
    (recipe on Page 51)
Chili Toppings:
1 cup shredded Cheddar cheese
1 cup shredded Monterey Jack cheese
2 cups shredded lettuce
1 cup sour cream
1 cup chopped green onions

Combine ground beef, onion, green pepper and garlic in a Dutch oven. Cook over medium heat until beef is browned, stirring to crumble meat. Remove excess fat. Add water, beans, tomato paste, tomatoes, olives, jalapeno pepper, chili powder, brown sugar, salt, garlic salt, cumin and black pepper. Mix well. Cover and simmer 1½ hours.

Meanwhile, prepare Cheese Bread Bowls. Serve chili in warm bread bowls.

Place desired Chili Toppings in separate small bowls. Guests may choose one or all of the toppings for their chili.

Makes 8 servings.

Veal Mushroom Swiss Steak

1 (1 1/2 pound) boneless veal round steak, cut 1/2-inch thick
1 tablespoon olive oil
Salt and coarsely ground black pepper to taste
1/3 cup dry white wine
1/2 pound small mushrooms, cut in half
2 medium tomatoes, seeded and diced
1/3 cup finely chopped fresh basil

Cut veal steak into 6 pieces. Using a meat mallet, pound steak to ¼-inch thickness.

Heat oil in a 12-inch, nonstick skillet. Add veal, a few pieces at a time. Brown on both sides. Remove veal and keep warm. When all of the veal is browned, return it to the skillet. Season with salt and pepper. Cook over medium heat 4 to 5 minutes, or until tender. Turn meat occasionally. Transfer veal to a serving platter; keep warm.

Add wine and mushrooms to skillet, scraping browned bits from bottom of pan. Cook over medium-high heat, stirring frequently, about 3 minutes, or until mushrooms are tender. Add tomatoes and basil; heat through. Spoon vegetable mixture and pan juices over steak.

Makes 6 servings.

Blueberry Sauced Veal Medallions

1 cup fresh or frozen blueberries
1/4 cup all-purpose flour
1/4 teaspoon paprika
1/4 teaspoon ground white pepper
1/4 teaspoon salt
4 veal medallions (4 ounces each)
1 tablespoon butter
1 teaspoon minced garlic
2 teaspoon chopped fresh sage
1/4 cup chicken stock
2 tablespoons dry white wine
Fresh sage leaves for garnish

Rinse and drain blueberries; set aside. On a piece of waxed paper, combine flour, paprika, white pepper and salt; mix well.

Lightly dust veal medallions with seasoned flour. In large skillet, melt butter; saute veal over medium-high heat until golden brown on both sides. Do not overcook. Veal should be slightly pink. Arrange veal on serving plate and place in warming oven. Add garlic, chopped sage, chicken stock and wine to skillet. Bring sauce to a simmer, then add blueberries. Continue cooking, stirring gently, until blueberries are heated through. Pour sauce over veal. Garnish with sage leaves.

Makes 4 servings.

Mushroom Stuffed Veal Breast

4 teaspoons olive oil, divided
1 1/2 cups chopped mushrooms
1/2 cup finely chopped red bell pepper
2 cloves garlic, peeled
   and finely chopped
1/2 teaspoon dried rosemary, crushed
1 (2 1/2 to 3 pounds) boneless
   veal breast
1/2 teaspoon salt
1/3 cup dry red wine
1/3 cup water

Heat 2 teaspoons oil in a 10-inch, nonstick skillet. Add mushrooms, pepper and garlic. Cook over medium heat 5 minutes, or until mushrooms are tender. Stir in rosemary. Remove from heat; let cool.

Unroll veal breast; trim excess surface fat. Sprinkle evenly with salt. Spread cooled mushroom mixture evenly over surface. Roll up veal breast, tying securely with string.

Heat remaining 2 teaspoons oil in a Dutch oven. Cook veal over medium heat until all sides are brown. Add wine and water. Cover and simmer over low heat 1 hour and 30 minutes to 1 hour and 45 minutes, or until veal is tender. Transfer veal to platter; keep warm. Skim fat from pan juices, if necessary. Cook over high heat until reduced by one-third. Slice veal, discarding string. Spoon sauce over each serving.

Makes 6 servings.

Pork Medallions with Rosemary and Mushrooms

1 pound pork tenderloin, trimmed and cut into 8 crosswise pieces
1 tablespoon butter or margarine
1 cup sliced fresh mushrooms
2 tablespoons finely chopped onion
1 to 3 teaspoons chopped fresh rosemary or 1 teaspoon dried rosemary leaves, crushed
1/4 teaspoon celery salt
1/4 teaspoon ground black pepper
1 clove garlic, peeled and minced
1 tablespoon dry vermouth or sherry
Fresh rosemary sprigs for garnish, optional
Fresh mushroom caps for garnish, optional

Press each slice of pork to 1-inch thickness. Melt butter in a large, heavy skillet over medium-high heat. Brown pork slices quickly, about 1 minute on each side. Remove from heat. Place cooked pork slices on a serving platter, reserving pan drippings. Keep warm.

Add mushrooms, onion, rosemary, celery salt, pepper and garlic to reserved drippings in the skillet. Cook over low heat about 2 minutes, stirring frequently. Add vermouth; stir to blend. Return pork slices to skillet; spoon mushroom mixture over slices. Cover and simmer 3 to 4 minutes. Place pork slices and mushroom mixture on serving platter. Garnish with sprigs of fresh rosemary and mushroom caps, if desired.

Makes 4 servings.

Baked Ham with Sugared Plums

4 slices cooked ham
1/2 cup granulated sugar
1 teaspoon ground cinnamon
1/4 cup butter or margarine, melted
4 large ripe plums, halved and pitted

Brown ham slices on both sides in a large skillet; keep warm.

In a small bowl, combine sugar and cinnamon. Dip plum halves in melted butter, then in sugar mixture.

Place plums in a circle on a microwave-safe plate. Cover with waxed paper. Microwave on HIGH (100% power) 2 to 3 minutes, or until fork tender. Do not overcook because plums will lose their shape. Let stand 1 to 2 minutes. Serve plums with ham slices.

Makes 4 servings.

Right: Baked Ham with Sugared Plums

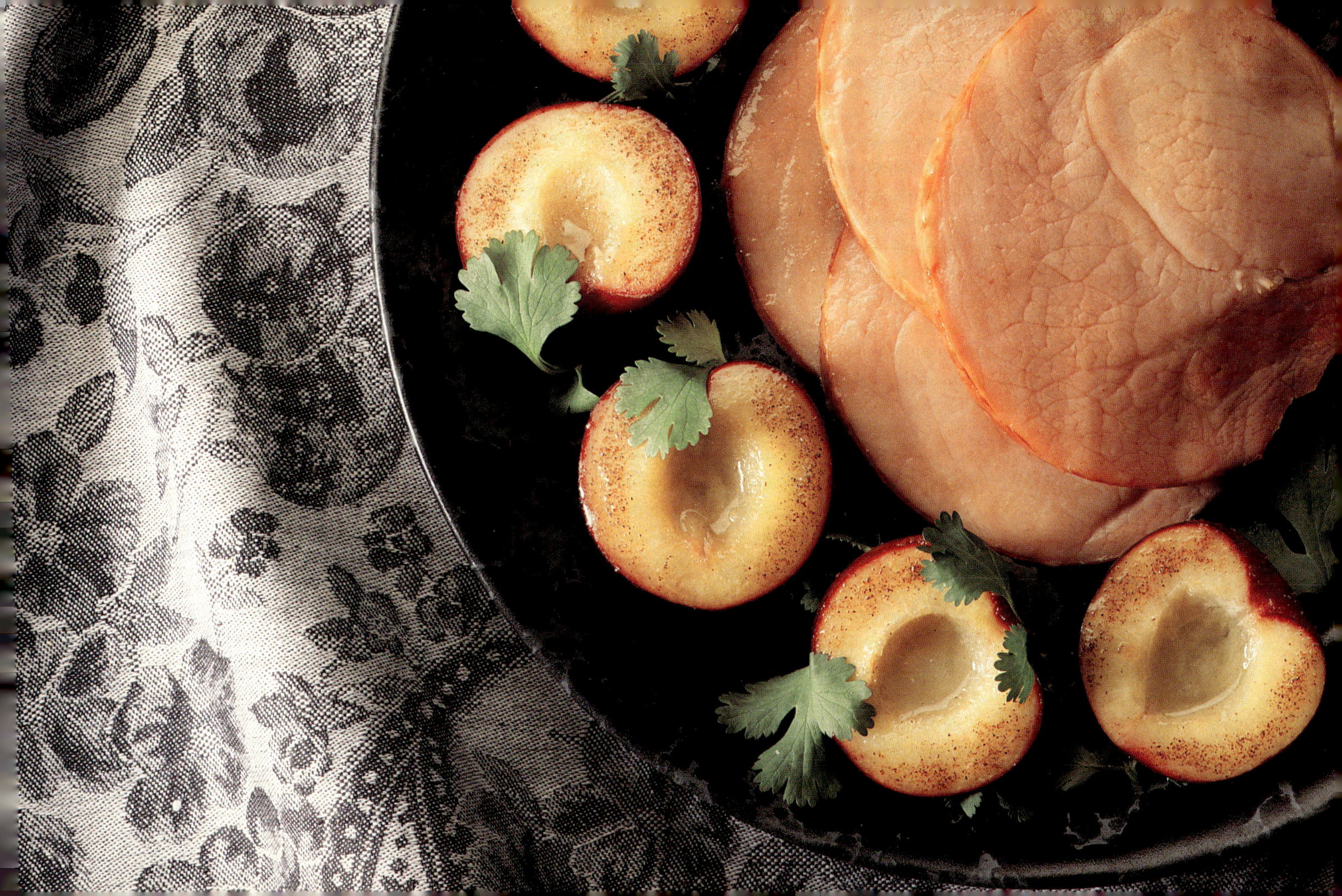

Maple Barbecued Spareribs

3 pounds baby-back pork spareribs
3/4 cup pure maple syrup
1 tablespoon ketchup
1 tablespoon cider vinegar
1 tablespoon finely chopped onion
1 teaspoon Worcestershire sauce
1 teaspoon salt
1/4 teaspoon dry mustard
1/8 teaspoon ground black pepper

Place spareribs in a large saucepot or Dutch oven. Add enough water to cover. Bring to a boil over high heat. Reduce heat; simmer 30 minutes. Drain.

In a small bowl, combine maple syrup, ketchup, vinegar, onion, Worcestershire sauce, salt, mustard and black pepper. Mix well.

Place spareribs in a shallow baking pan. Brush about half of the maple syrup sauce over the ribs. Bake in a preheated 350-degree oven 30 minutes, or until spareribs are tender. While ribs are baking, turn them occasionally and baste with remaining maple syrup sauce. Broil 5 minutes to brown ribs.

Makes 4 servings.

Burgundy Lamb Chops

2 tablespoons vegetable oil
8 lamb loin or rib chops,
    cut 1-inch thick
1 medium onion, coarsely chopped
2 cloves garlic, minced
1 teaspoon coarsely ground
    black pepper
8 ounces fresh mushrooms,
    thinly sliced
1 cup dry red wine
2 tablespoons cornstarch
1/4 cup cold water

Heat oil in large skillet. Add lamb chops, onion, garlic and pepper. Cook, uncovered, 10 minutes, turning once. Transfer chops to platter; keep warm. Add mushrooms and wine. Cook, 5 minutes, or until tender. Combine cornstarch and water; stir into mushroom mixture. Cook 2 to 3 minutes, or until thickened. Serve over chops.

Makes 4 servings.

Stuffed Lamb with Honey Glaze

1 bunch fresh spinach
1/4 cup plus 1 tablespoon olive oil, divided
1 medium onion, finely chopped
1/2 cup finely chopped fresh parsley
3 large cloves garlic, peeled and finely chopped
1/2 teaspoon dried oregano, crumbled
1/8 teaspoon cayenne pepper
1/2 cup fine dry bread crumbs
1 egg, lightly beaten
1 (5 to 6 pound) leg of lamb, boned and butterflied
2 teaspoon lemon juice
Salt and ground black pepper to taste
5 ounces chevre (goat cheese)
2 tablespoons honey

Rinse spinach carefully; remove stems. Steam spinach in a large saucepan until just wilted. Drain well, then chop and drain again. Set aside.

In a large skillet, heat 1/4 cup olive oil. Add onion, parsley, garlic, oregano and cayenne. Cook over medium heat, stirring occasionally, until onion is tender. Add chopped spinach; saute 3 minutes. Remove skillet from heat and let mixture cool, then add bread crumbs and egg; mix well. Set aside.

Place the lamb on a work surface, fat side down, and flatten it as much as possible. Rub with remaining 1 tablespoon olive oil and lemon juice. Sprinkle with salt and pepper. Spread spinach mixture evenly over lamb. Sprinkle chevre evenly over spinach mixture. Carefully roll lamb, enclosing the spinach mixture. Tie securely. Coat the top and sides of the rolled and tied roast with honey.

Place lamb on a rack in a roasting pan. Bake in a preheated 425-degree oven 10 minutes. Reduce oven temperature to 375 degrees; continue roasting about 1 hour and 30 minutes for medium rare. Remove pan from oven and let roast cool 15 minutes before carving and serving.

Makes 8 to 10 servings.

Roast Lamb with Mint Sauce

1 (1 1/4 pound) Frenched 6 to 7-bone baby rack of lamb
3/4 teaspoon grated fresh gingerroot
1/4 teaspoon dried whole rosemary
1 cup apple cider
1 tablespoon honey
1/4 teaspoon coarsely ground black pepper
Mint Sauce (recipe follows)

Rub meaty portion of lamb with gingerroot and rosemary. Place lamb in a shallow roasting pan; add cider. Bake in a 450-degree oven 20 minutes. Drizzle honey over lamb. Continue baking 10 to 12 minutes, or to desired degree of doneness.

Place lamb on serving platter. Sprinkle with pepper. Cover with foil. Let roast stand 10 minutes before carving into individual chops. Serve with Mint Sauce.

Makes 2 to 3 servings.

Mint Sauce:
2 tablespoons brown sugar
1/4 cup cider vinegar
2 tablespoons water
1/3 cup apple jelly
1/4 cup finely chopped, fresh mint leaves

In a small saucepan, combine brown sugar, vinegar and water. Cook, stirring occasionally, over medium heat until mixture is reduced by one-third. Stir in jelly; cook over low heat until jelly is melted. Stir in mint. Let cool before serving with roast lamb.

Makes ¾ cup sauce.

Turkey with Cherry Wine Sauce

1 (12 to 14 pound) turkey, thawed if frozen
Vegetable oil
1/4 cup granulated sugar
1 1/2 tablespoons cornstarch
1 teaspoon dry mustard
1 teaspoon ground ginger
1/4 teaspoon salt
1/2 cup cherry wine
1/2 cup orange juice
1/4 cup currant jelly
1 pound frozen, tart cherries, thawed and drained OR
   1 (16-ounce) can tart cherries, drained
2 tablespoons brandy, optional

Remove neck and giblets from turkey cavities. Rinse well and pat dry. Place turkey, breast side up, on a flat rack in an open pan. Insert meat thermometer deep into thickest part of thigh, not touching bone. Brush skin with oil. Bake turkey in a 325-degree oven about 4 hours. Check for doneness; thigh temperature should be 180 to 185 degrees. Let turkey stand 15 to 20 minutes before carving.

Meanwhile, in a sauce pan, combine sugar, cornstarch, dry mustard, ginger and salt. Add cherry wine, orange juice and jelly. Cook, stirring constantly, over medium heat until thickened. Add cherries and brandy. Continue cooking sauce 1 to 2 minutes, or until cherries are hot. Do not overcook. Serve sauce with slices of turkey.

Makes 8 to 10 servings.

Note: Any roast game bird including duck, goose and Cornish game hens is excellent with the cherry sauce.

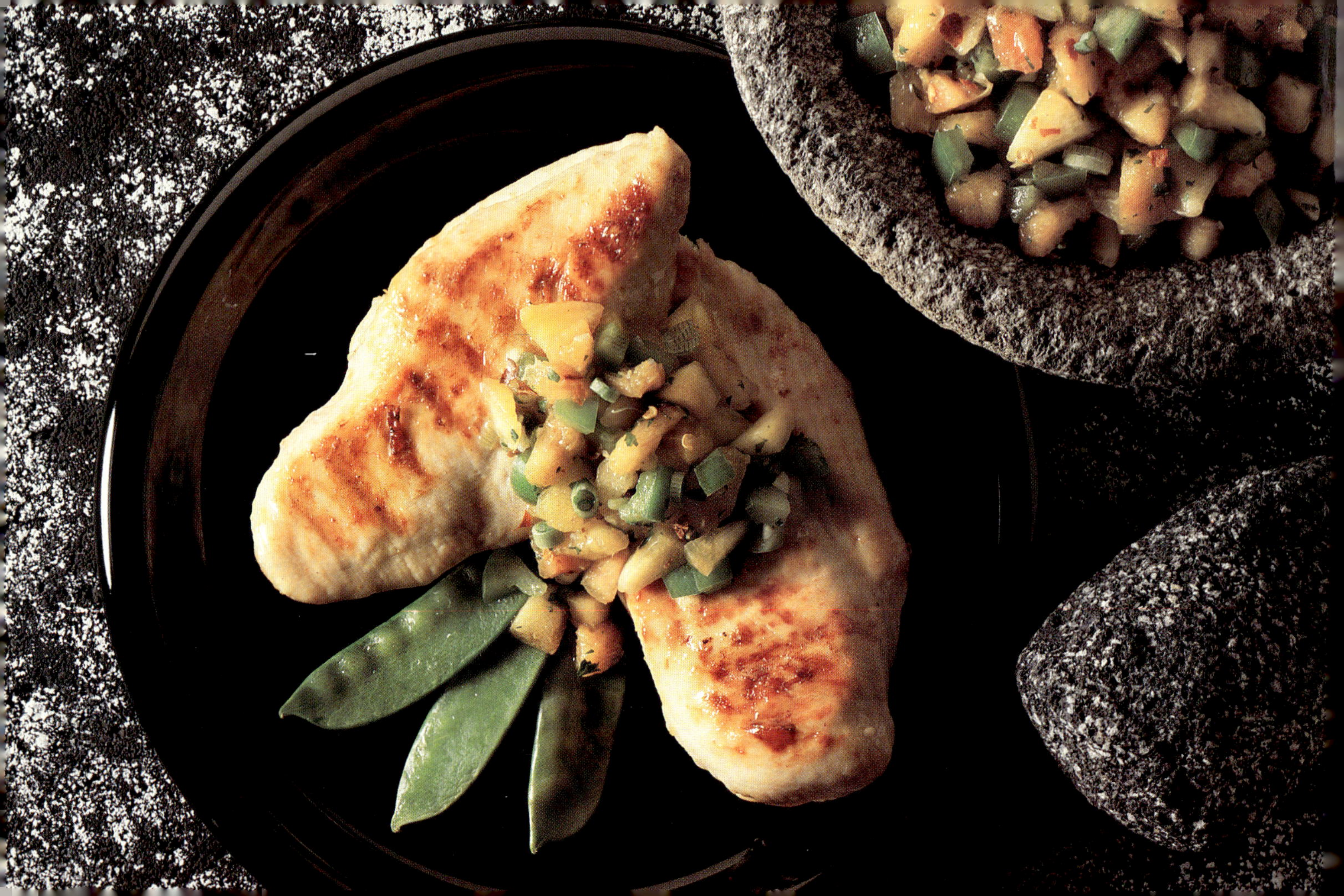

Grilled Chicken with Peach Salsa

6 ripe peaches (about 2 pounds)
1 large green bell pepper
2 green onions, thinly sliced
3 tablespoons finely chopped cilantro or parsley
2 tablespoons lime juice
2 cloves garlic, peeled and crushed
1/4 teaspoon red pepper flakes
Salt and ground black pepper to taste
8 grilled chicken breast halves

Pare and pit peaches; chop into ¼-inch pieces. Core and seed pepper; chop into ¼-inch pieces.

In a large mixing bowl, combine peaches, green pepper, green onion, cilantro or parsley, lime juice, garlic and red pepper flakes. Mix well. Season with salt and black pepper.

Cover and let stand at room temperature at least 2 hours or refrigerate at least 4 hours to blend flavors. Serve with grilled chicken.

Makes 4 cups of salsa; 4 servings chicken.

Variations: Peach Salsa is also good with grilled fish or chops, or as an appetizer atop a small round of Brie cheese.

Left: Grilled Chicken with Peach Salsa and Fresh Garden Pea Pods

Hot Chicken and Celery Salad

3 cups chopped cooked chicken
1 1/2 cups sliced celery
1 cup (4 ounces) shredded sharp
　　Cheddar cheese, divided
1 tablespoon grated onion
1 tablespoon lemon juice
Salt and ground black pepper to taste
About 1/2 cup mayonnaise
3 tomato slices
1 1/2 cups crushed potato chips

In a large mixing bowl, combine chicken, celery, ½ cup cheese, onion and lemon juice; mix well. Season with salt and pepper. Add enough mayonnaise to moisten; mix lightly. Spoon chicken mixture into a lightly greased 1 ½-quart casserole; top with tomato slices.

Bake in a 350-degree oven 35 minutes. Combine remaining ½ cup cheese and crushed potato chips. Sprinkle chip mixture over casserole; continue baking 5 to 10 minutes, or until cheese is melted.

Makes 6 servings.

Fish Fillets with Garden Vegetables

1 pound whitefish fillets
5 green onions, sliced
1 medium zucchini,
　　cut into 1/4-inch slices
1 medium yellow summer squash,
　　cut into 1/4-inch slices
1/2 pound mushrooms,
　　rinsed and sliced
3 tablespoons butter or margarine,
　　melted
1 teaspoon lemon juice
1/2 teaspoon dried oregano, crushed
1/4 teaspoon salt
1/8 teaspoon ground black pepper
1 medium tomato, rinsed and cored

　　Rinse fish fillets well and pat dry. Arrange fish fillets with thickest parts to the outside edge of an 11x7x2-inch microwave-safe container. Top with onions, zucchini, squash and mushrooms. Combine butter, lemon juice, oregano, salt and pepper. Pour butter mixture over fish.
　　Microwave, covered, on HIGH (100% power) 4 minutes. Rotate dish ½ turn. Remove excess liquid from baking dish. Continue to microwave on HIGH 6 minutes, or until fish flakes easily with a fork and vegetables are crisp-tender. Remove excess liquid from baking dish. Cut tomato into 8 wedges; add to fish. Cover and microwave on HIGH 1 to 2 minutes, or until tomato wedges are hot. Do not overcook.
　　Makes 4 servings.

Planked Whitefish

2 pounds potatoes, peeled and quartered
9 tablespoons butter or margarine, divided
3 tablespoons milk
Salt and ground black pepper to taste
2 pounds (1 or 2 fillets) boneless whitefish
Paprika to taste

In a large saucepan over high heat, cook potatoes in water until boiling. Reduce heat; simmer until potatoes are tender. Drain well. Mash potatoes well. Beat in 6 tablespoons butter and milk. Season with salt and pepper. Put mashed potatoes into a pastry bag with a wide tip.

Preheat broiler. Select a oven-proof serving platter just large enough to hold the fish. (If using 2 fillets, they may be placed on separate platters or on the same platter next to each other.)

Rinse fish fillets and pat dry. Place fish on platter. Melt remaining 3 tablespoons butter; brush over fish. Sprinkle with paprika.

Pipe potatoes around the edge of the fish, covering the entire platter. Broil, 5 to 6 inches from heat, until fish flakes easily when tested with a fork and potatoes are lightly browned. Serve immediately, taking care in handling the hot platter.

Makes 4 servings.

Vegetables

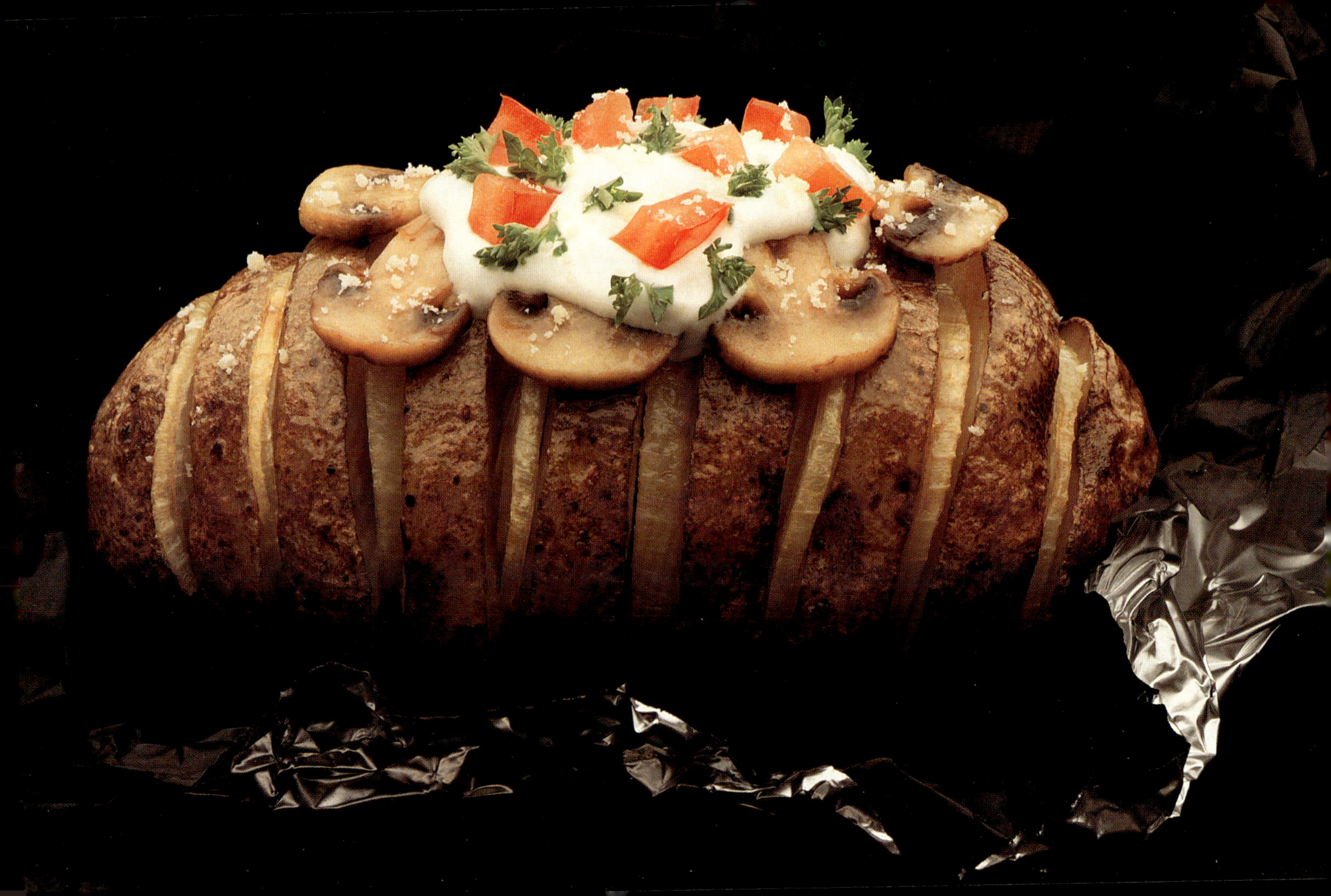

Grilled Stuffed Potato

4 large baking potatoes,
   washed and scrubbed
4 medium onions,
   peeled and thinly sliced
2 cups fresh mushrooms, sliced
1/4 cup butter or margarine
1/2 teaspoon seasoned salt
1/4 teaspoon garlic powder
1/4 teaspoon celery salt
1/8 teaspoon ground black pepper
1 tablespoon fresh chopped parsley
1/4 cup grated Parmesan cheese
1 large chopped tomato
1 cup sour cream

Slice potatoes crosswise at ¼-inch intervals, leaving deep slits, but not cutting through the potato. Place an onion slice in each slit.

Place each potato on a piece of aluminum foil large enough to wrap the potato. Top each potato with a portion of sliced mushrooms.

In a small saucepan, heat butter, seasoned salt, garlic powder, celery salt and pepper. Mix well after butter melts. Pour butter mixture evenly over all the potatoes.

Wrap potatoes securely with foil. Bake on an outdoor grill over direct heat or in a preheated 375-degree oven 55 to 60 minutes, or until potatoes are cooked.

To serve, open packet and top potatoes with parsley, Parmesan cheese, tomatoes and sour cream.

Makes 4 servings.

Left: Grilled Stuffed Potato

Potato Wedges

4 medium potatoes,
   each cut into 8 wedges
Vegetable oil
Seasoned salt
3/4 cup sour cream
1/3 cup shredded Cheddar cheese

Place potato wedges, cut sides down, on lightly oiled baking sheet. Brush potatoes with oil; sprinkle with seasoned salt. Broil, 3 to 4 inches from heat, 5 to 6 minutes, or until golden brown. Turn; brush with oil and sprinkle with seasoned salt. Broil 5 minutes, or until potatoes are golden brown and tender.

Spoon sour cream in center of a large serving platter; sprinkle with cheese. Arrange potato wedges around sour cream.

Makes 4 side dishes or 8 appetizer servings.

Herbed New Potatoes

12 medium new potatoes
2 tablespoons water
3 tablespoons butter or margarine
2 tablespoons finely chopped
    fresh parsley
1 tablespoons lemon juice
1 1/2 teaspoons finely chopped fresh
    dill or 1/2 teaspoon dried
    dillweed, crushed
1 teaspoon chopped chives

Rinse potatoes. Prick each potato twice with a fork. Place potatoes in a 2-quart microwave-safe dish. Add water. Microwave, covered, on HIGH (100% power) 8 to 10 minutes, stirring after 4 minutes. Let potatoes stand 3 to 4 minutes. (Or cook potatoes, covered with water, in a saucepan on top of the range until tender.)

Meanwhile, place butter in a 1-cup microwave-safe container. Microwave on HIGH 30 seconds, or until butter is melted. Stir in parsley, lemon juice, dill and chives. (Or melt butter in a saucepan and stir in parsley, lemon juice, dill and chives.)

Drain potatoes. Pour butter mixture over potatoes. Serve immediately.

Makes 4 to 6 servings.

Baked Celery

1 bunch celery
3 tablespoons butter or margarine
3 tablespoons all-purpose flour
1/2 teaspoon salt
1/4 teaspoon ground black pepper
1 1/2 cups milk
1 can (8 ounces) sliced water chestnuts, drained and rinsed
Seasoned Crumb Topping (recipe follows)

Rinse celery stalks in cold water and cut each stalk into ½-inch slices; set aside.

Melt butter in a small saucepan. Remove from heat and blend in flour, salt and pepper. Gradually add milk. Cook over medium heat, stirring constantly, until mixture is thickened and bubbly. Remove from heat. Stir in celery and water chestnuts. Turn mixture into a greased 1-quart baking dish. Top with Seasoned Crumb Topping.

Bake in a preheated 350-degree oven 20 to 25 minutes, or until hot and bubbly.

Makes 4 to 6 servings.

SEASONED CRUMB TOPPING:
1/2 cup dry bread crumbs
2 tablespoons butter or margarine, melted
1/8 teaspoon salt
1/8 teaspoon garlic powder
1/8 teaspoon dried thyme
1/8 teaspoon dried basil
1/8 teaspoon dried oregano
1 tablespoon chopped fresh parsley

In a small mixing bowl, combine bread crumbs, butter, salt, garlic, thyme, basil, oregano and parsley. Use to top celery casserole.

Marinated Asparagus

2 to 3 pounds fresh asparagus
2 quarts water
1/2 dill pickle, chopped
1 tablespoon finely chopped onion
1/2 cup olive oil or other vegetable oil
2 tablespoons red wine vinegar
1 teaspoon lemon juice
1 teaspoon granulated sugar
1 teaspoon salt
1/2 teaspoon freshly ground black pepper
1/4 teaspoon dry mustard
1 tablespoon finely chopped, fresh parsley
1 tablespoon finely chopped pimiento
1 tablespoon finely chopped, hard-cooked egg white
Leaf lettuce, rinsed and well drained
1 pint cherry tomatoes

Clean asparagus, then break off and discard ends. Cut remaining stalks into 1½-inch pieces. Bring 2 quarts of water to a boil in a large saucepot. Add asparagus and blanch 1 to 2 minutes, or until asparagus is just tender. Rinse in cold water; refrigerate immediately to cool asparagus.

To make vinaigrette dressing, combine pickle, onion, oil, vinegar, lemon juice, sugar, salt, pepper and mustard. Let dressing stand at least 30 minutes. Add parsley, pimiento and egg white to dressing; mix well.

Pour vinaigrette dressing over asparagus and toss gently. Line a large serving bowl with lettuce. Arrange asparagus on lettuce and place tomatoes in a ring around the edge of the salad.

Makes 10 servings.

Broiled Tomatoes with Chevre

4 medium tomatoes, rinsed and cored
3 ounces chevre (goat cheese), cut into 16 thin slices
3 tablespoons chopped fresh basil
Freshly ground black pepper

Slice each tomato into 4 thick slices. Arrange in a single layer in a shallow baking dish. Place chevre slices over tomato slices. Sprinkle basil evenly over cheese. Season with pepper to taste. Broil 2 to 3 minutes, or until cheese melts.

Makes 8 servings.

Note: If desired, microwave tomato slices on HIGH (100% power) 2 minutes, or until cheese melts.

Corn and Noodle Casserole

2 cups egg noodles
1/2 cup sliced fresh mushrooms
2 tablespoons butter or margarine
1 tablespoon all-purpose flour
1 teaspoon salt, optional
1/4 teaspooon chili powder
1/4 teaspoon ground black pepper
1 cup milk
1 cup shredded Cheddar cheese, divided
1 can (16 ounces) cream-style corn
1 jar (2 ounces) chopped pimiento

Cook egg noodles according to package directions; drain and set aside.

In a large saucepan, combine mushrooms and butter. Cook over medium heat until butter is melted and mushroooms are tender. Stir in flour, salt, chili powder and pepper; mix well. Remove from heat and gradually stir in milk. Cook over medium heat, stirring constantly, until thickened.

Add ½ cup cheese, corn, cooked noodles and pimiento. Pour into a greased 2-quart casserole. Top with remaining ½ cup cheese. Bake in a preheated 350-degree oven 30 minutes, or until hot and bubbly.

Makes 6 to 8 servings.

Hot Peppery Corn-on-the Cob

1/2 cup butter or margarine, softened
3 tablespoons sliced green onions
1 tablespoon snipped chives
1/4 teaspoon freshly ground black pepper
1/4 teaspoon chili powder
1/4 teaspoon ground white pepper
1/4 teaspoon cayenne pepper, optional
8 ears cooked corn-on-the-cob

In a small mixing bowl, combine butter, green onions, chives, black pepper, chili powder, white pepper and cayenne; mix well. Spread on hot, cooked corn-on-the-cob.

Makes 8 servings.

Note: Butter mixture may be stored in the refrigerator 5 to 7 days.

Confetti Peppers

4 medium green bell peppers
1 1/2 cups cooked corn
   (fresh, frozen or canned)
1/2 cup finely chopped cooked ham
1/2 cup finely chopped onion
2 cups soft bread crumbs, divided
1 cup finely chopped tomato
1/4 cup butter or margarine
1/4 cup water

Cut the tops off peppers; seed, rinse, and drain them. Fill a large saucepot or Dutch oven with water. Bring to a boil. Add peppers and boil 2 to 3 minutes. Do not overcook peppers; they will continue to cook while baking. Drain peppers well; set aside.

In a large mixing bowl, combine corn, ham, onion, 1 cup bread crumbs and tomatoes; mix well. Fill each pepper half with a generous portion of corn mixture. Sprinkle remaining 1 cup bread crumbs over corn-stuffed peppers. Dot with butter. Place peppers in baking dish. Pour ¼ cup water in pan around peppers. Bake in a preheated 350-degree oven 35 to 40 minutes, or until peppers are tender and corn mixture is hot.

Makes 4 servings.

Honey Glazed Carrots

8 medium carrots, peeled
   and cut into julienne strips
3/4 cup water
2 teaspoon granulated sugar
1/4 cup honey
2 tablespoons orange juice
2 tablespoons butter or margarine
Salt to taste

In a medium saucepan, combine carrots, water and sugar. Cook, covered, 5 to 8 minutes, or until carrots are crisp-tender. Drain carrots, reserving ¼ cup cooking liquid. Set aside carrots.

In a small saucepan, combine reserved cooking liquid, honey, orange juice and butter. Season with salt. Bring mixture to a boil; continue cooking 5 minutes. Add carrots; reduce heat and simmer 2 to 3 minutes. Serve immediately.

Makes 4 to 6 servings.

Desserts

Apple Dumplings With Dried Cherries

3 1/2 cups all-purpose flour
1 tablespoon granulated sugar
1 1/4 cups butter, divided
1/3 cup solid vegetable shortening
1/3 cup cold water
2/3 cup peach preserves
1/2 cup pure maple syrup
1/4 cup brandy
1/2 teaspoon ground cinnamon
1/2 cup dried cherries
2/3 cup white wine
6 medium baking apples, such as
   Pippin or Paula Red
2 tablespoons lemon juice
6 whole cloves
1 egg yolk
1 teaspoon water

In a large mixing bowl, combine flour and sugar; mix well. Cut in 1 cup butter and shortening with a pastry blender or fork until mixture resembles coarse crumbs. Add just enough cold water to form a dough that holds together. Knead quickly on a floured surface, leaving small visible pieces of butter. Do not overwork the dough. Wrap dough in waxed paper; let chill while preparing apples.

In a small saucepan, combine preserves, syrup, remaining ¼ cup butter, brandy and cinnamon. Cook over low heat until butter is melted.

In another small saucepan, combine dried cherries and wine. Simmer 10 minutes. Remove from heat and let steep.

Core apples with corer, leaving a 1-inch opening. Pare apples; brush with lemon juice. Drain cherries, reserving liquid. Fill center of each apple with cherries, then spoon about 3 tablespoons peach mixture over cherries in each apple. Pour reserved cherry liquid into remaining peach mixture and set aside.

On a lightly floured pastry cloth, divide pastry into 6 equal pieces. Form each piece into a round ball. Flatten each ball, then roll out from the center into an 8½-inch square. Trim edges, using pastry wheel to make a decorative edge. Save trimmings.

Carefully place an apple in the center of each pastry square making sure filling does not fall out. Brush edges of pastry lightly with water. Bring each corner of the pastry square to top of apple; pinch edges of pastry together firmly to cover apple completely.

Reroll trimmings ¼-inch thick. With a

sharp knife, cut out 24 leaves. With the edge of knife, make indentation to look like the veins of the leaves. Brush the bottom of one end of each leaf with water. Press ends of 4 leaves into top of one pastry-covered apple; press clove in center to form stem of apple. Repeat with remaining apples. In a small container, combine egg yolk and water; mix well. Brush pastry-covered apples completely with egg yolk mixture.

Bake on a lightly greased baking sheet in a preheated 375-degree oven 40 minutes, or until pastry is golden brown. Serve warm with remaining peach mixture.

Makes 6 servings.

Right: Apple Dumpling with Dried Cherries

Snowcap Blueberry Ice Cream Pie

1 (8 or 9 inch) graham cracker crust
1 quart vanilla ice cream, softened
1 1/2 cups Blueberry Honey Sauce
   (recipe at right)
3 egg whites
1/2 teaspoon vanilla extract
1/4 teaspoon cream of tartar, optional
6 tablespoons granulated sugar

Spread one-half of the ice cream into graham cracker crust. In a mixing bowl, combine remaining ice cream and Blueberry Honey Sauce; mix well. Pour over vanilla ice cream layer. Freeze 4 to 6 hours, or until firm.

When almost ready to serve, prepare meringue. Allow egg whites to reach room temperature. Beat egg whites, vanilla and cream of tartar until soft peaks form. Gradually add sugar, beating until stiff and glossy.

Remove pie from freezer. Cover entire surface of ice cream with meringue, sealing to edges. Place pie on a baking sheet. Bake in a preheated 475-degree oven 2 to 3 minutes, or until lightly browned. Serve immediately.

Makes 6 to 8 servings.

Blueberry Honey Sauce

2 cups fresh or frozen blueberries
1/2 cup honey
1/4 cup unsalted butter
1 teaspoon ground cinnamon
1/2 teaspoon freshly grated nutmeg
Dash of salt

If using fresh blueberries, rinse and drain them well. If using frozen blueberries, it is not necessary to thaw them.

In a saucepan, combine, blueberries, honey and butter. Season with cinnamon, nutmeg and salt. Bring mixture to a boil over high heat. Reduce heat, then simmer 5 minutes, stirring occasionally. Use sauce to make Blueberry Ice Cream Pie or as a topping on ice cream or frozen yogurt.

Makes 1 ½ cups sauce.

Traverse Bay Cherry-Nut Cake

1 cup vegetable oil
1 cup granulated sugar
1 cup cherry applesauce
    or regular applesauce
1 cup mashed ripe bananas
    (2 medium bananas)
3 eggs
3 cups all-purpose flour
1/2 teaspoon salt
1/2 teaspoon baking powder
1 teaspoon baking soda
1 teaspoon ground cinnamon
1 teaspoon ground ginger
1/2 teaspoon ground nutmeg
1 cup dried cherries
1 1/2 cups chopped pecans, divided
Cream Cheese Frosting (recipe follows)

In a large mixing bowl with an electric mixer, combine oil and sugar. Add applesauce, banana and eggs; mix well.

In another bowl, combine flour, salt, baking powder, baking soda, cinnamon, ginger and nutmeg. Gradually add flour mixture to egg mixture, beating well after each addition. Stir in cherries and ½ cup pecans. Pour batter into 2 greased, 9-inch round baking pans.

Bake in a preheated 350-degree oven 30 minutes, or until wooden pick inserted into cake comes out clean. Remove cake from pans and let cool on wire racks. Frost cake with Cream Cheese Frosting, then gently press remaining 1 cup pecans around outside edges of cake.

Makes 10 to 12 servings.

Cream Cheese Frosting
1 package (8 ounces) cream cheese, softened
1/2 cup butter or margarine, softened
1 box (16 ounces) confectioners' sugar, sifted (about 4 cups)
1 teaspoon vanilla extract

In a medium mixing bowl with an electric mixer, combine cream cheese and butter. Beat until smooth. Gradually add confectioners' sugar. Beat until light and fluffy. Add vanilla; mix well. Use to frost Cherry-Nut Cake.

Cherries Jubilee

1 can (16 ounces) dark sweet cherries in heavy syrup
1 tablespoon cornstarch
1/4 teaspoon ground cinnamon
1/8 teaspoon ground nutmeg
2 to 4 tablespoons cherry brandy
Ice cream or pound cake

Drain syrup from cherries into a medium saucepan; set cherries aside. Add cornstarch, cinnamon and nutmeg to cherry syrup. Stir until cornstarch is thoroughly dissolved. Cook over low heat until thickened and bubbly.

Add drained cherries; cook until cherries are hot.

Just before serving, heat brandy in a small container. Do not boil. Pour hot brandy over hot cherry mixture; carefully ignite. Stir until flames subside. Serve over ice cream or pound cake.

Makes 1½ cups sauce; 4 to 6 servings.

Chocolate Cherry Cheesecake

1 1/2 cups graham cracker crumbs
1/4 cup granulated sugar
1/4 cup finely chopped walnuts
1/3 cup butter or margarine, melted
2 packages (8 ounces each) cream cheese, softened
1 cup granulated sugar
3 tablespoons all-purpose flour
2 teaspoons vanilla extract
1 teaspoon almond extract
3 eggs, slightly beaten
1 container (24 ounces) sour cream
1 cup frozen tart cherries, partially thawed, chopped and drained
   OR 1 can (16 ounce) tart cherries, chopped and drained
1/4 cup semisweet chocolate morsels

In a medium mixing bowl, combine graham cracker crumbs, sugar, walnuts and melted butter. Press onto the bottom and 2 inches up the sides of a 9-inch springform pan. Bake in a 375-degree oven 5 minutes. Set aside while preparing filling.

In a large mixing bowl with an electric mixer, beat cream cheese, sugar, flour, vanilla and almond extract until smooth and fluffy. Add eggs all at once; beat on low speed just until blended. Stir in sour cream, then fold in chopped cherries. Turn filling into crust.

Bake in a preheated 375-degree oven 55–65 minutes, or until the center appears almost set. Let cool on a wire rack 10 minutes. Loosen sides of pan and let cool completely, cover and refrigerate.

Before serving, melt chocolate morsels and drizzle over top and sides of cheesecake.

Makes 12 servings.

Orchard Streusel Cake

1/4 cup butter or margarine
3/4 cup granulated sugar
2 eggs, separated
1 1/2 cups all-purpose flour
1 teaspoon baking powder
1/2 cup milk
1 can (30 ounces) plums, drained or 2 cups fresh plums, sliced
1/2 cup firmly packed brown sugar
1 tablespoon butter or margarine, softened
1 teaspoon ground cinnamon
1/4 cup confectioners' sugar
1 teaspoon milk
1/4 teaspoon vanilla extract

In a large mixing bowl with an electric mixer, beat 1/4 cup butter, granulated sugar and egg yolks until light and fluffy. Combine flour and baking powder; beat into butter mixture alternately with 1/2 cup milk. In a separate bowl, beat egg whites until stiff but not dry. Fold beaten egg whites into butter mixture.

Pour batter into a lightly greased 9x9x2-inch baking pan. Halve and pit drained plums; arrange on top of batter.

Prepare streusel topping by combining brown sugar, 1 tablespoon butter and cinnamon; mix well. Sprinkle over plums.

Bake in a preheated 350-degree oven 35 to 40 minutes, or until top is golden and wooden pick inserted into cake comes out clean. Let cool on wire racks.

If desired, glaze cake by combining confectioners' sugar, 1 teaspoon milk and vanilla; mix well. Drizzle over cake.

Makes 8 to 10 servings.

Variations: Peaches, apples and pears may be used instead of the plums. For Peach Streusel Cake, use 2 fresh peaches, peeled and sliced into wedges or 1 can (14 ounces) sliced peaches, well drained. For Apple Streusel Cake, use 2 baking apples, sliced into thin wedges. For Pear Streusel Cake, use 2 pears, cored and thinly sliced or 1 can (14 ounces) sliced pears, well drained.

Raspberry Cream Cheese Torte

2 1/4 cups all-purpose flour
1 cup granulated sugar, divided
3/4 cup butter or margarine
1/2 teaspoon baking powder
1/2 teaspoon baking soda
1/4 teaspoon salt
3/4 cup sour cream
2 eggs
1 teaspoon almond extract
1 package (8 ounces) cream cheese, softened
1/2 cup raspberry preserves
1/2 cup sliced almonds

Grease and flour the bottom and sides of a 9-inch or 10-inch springform pan. Set aside.

In a large mixing bowl, combine flour and ¾ cup sugar. Cut butter into flour mixture with a pastry blender until mixture resembles coarse crumbs. Reserve 1 cup crumb mixture for later use. To remaining crumb mixture, add baking powder, baking soda and salt; mix well. Add sour cream, 1 egg and almond extract; blend well. Spread batter over bottom and 2 inches up the sides of prepared pan. (Batter should be about ¼-inch thick on the sides.)

In a small bowl with an electric mixer, combine cream cheese, remaining ¼ cup sugar and 1 egg; mix well. Pour over batter in pan. Carefully spoon preserves evenly over cheese filling.

In a small bowl, combine reserved crumb mixture and sliced almonds. Sprinkle over preserves.

Bake in a preheated 350-degree oven 45 to 55 minutes, or until cream cheese filling is set and crust is a deep golden brown. Let cool 15 minutes. Remove sides of pan. Serve warm or cooled. Refrigerate any leftovers.

Makes 16 servings.

Note: Peach, cherry or blueberry preserves may be substituted for the raspberry preserves.

Maple Fresh Fruit Cup

1 cup fresh sweet cherries, rinsed and pitted
2 peaches, peeled and cut into wedges
1 cup seedless grapes, rinsed and drained
2 pints strawberries, hulled, rinsed and drained
1 cup blueberries, rinsed and drained
3 tablespoons maple syrup

Prepare fruit within 3 hours of serving time. In a large serving bowl, combine cherries, peaches, grapes, strawberries and blueberries; toss to combine fruits.

Drizzle maple syrup over fruit; stir gently until mixed.

Makes 6 servings.

Right: Maple Fresh Fruit Cup

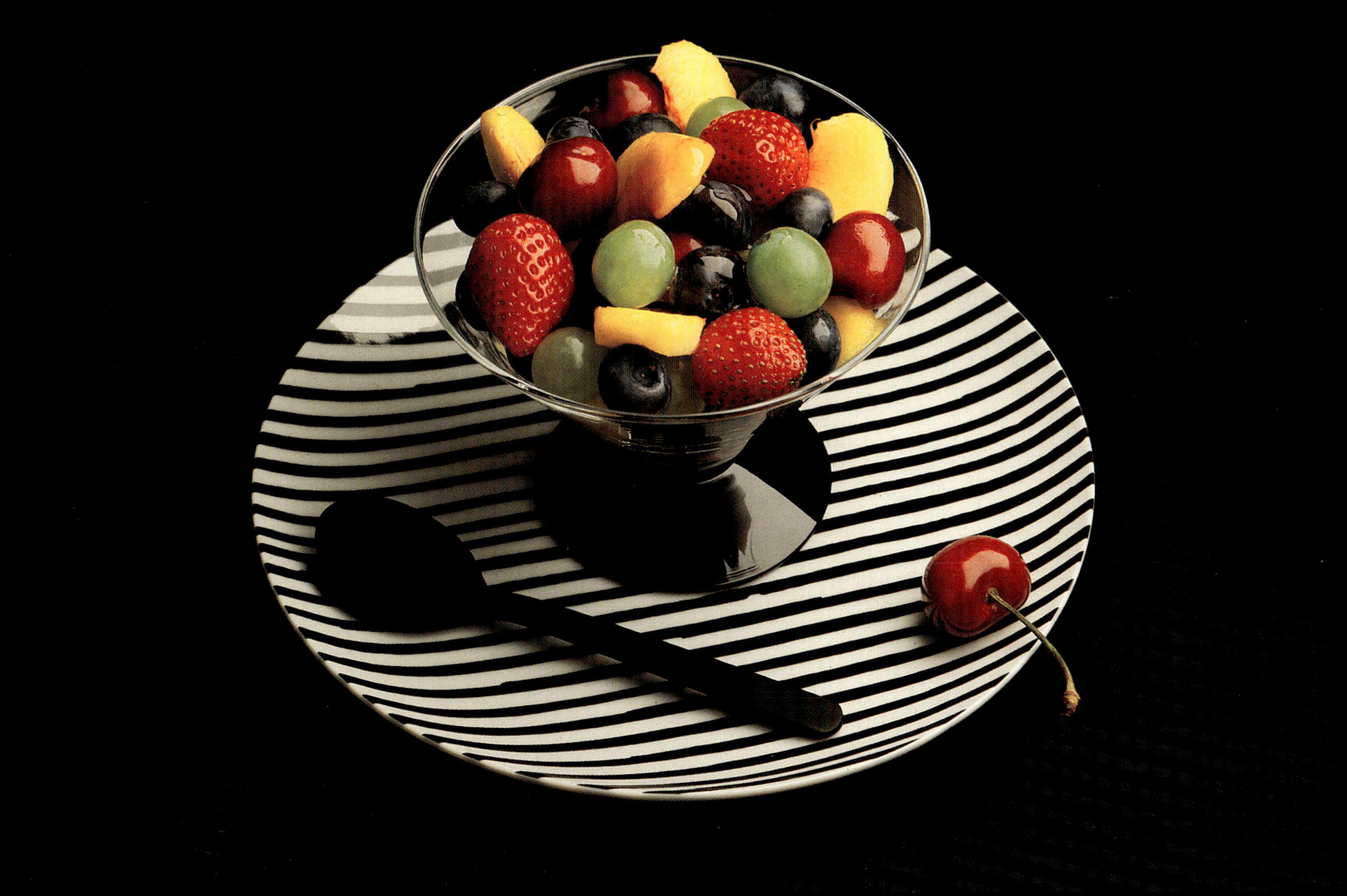

Cheesecake Squares

1/3 cup butter or margarine
1/3 cup firmly packed brown sugar
1 cup all-purpose flour
1/2 cup finely chopped walnuts
1 package (8 ounces) cream cheese, softened
1/4 cup granulated sugar
1 egg
1/2 teaspoon vanilla extract
2 tablespoons milk
1 tablespoon lemon juice

In a small mixing bowl with an electric mixer, beat butter and brown sugar until light and fluffy. With a fork, blend in flour until mixture resembles fine crumbs. Stir in walnuts. Reserve 1 cup flour mixture. Press remaining flour mixture into the bottom of a lightly greased 8x8x2-inch baking pan. Bake in a preheated 350-degree oven 12 to 15 minutes, or until golden brown.

Meanwhile, in another mixing bowl with an electric mixer, beat cream cheese and granulated sugar until fluffy. Add egg, vanilla, milk and lemon juice. Beat until smooth. Pour cream cheese mixture over baked crust. Sprinkle reserved flour mixture evenly over top.

Bake in a preheated 350-degree oven 20 minutes, or until cream cheese mixture is set and topping is golden brown. Let cool at room temperature, for 15 minutes, then chill in the refrigerator. To serve, cut into squares and remove from pan with a metal spatula.

Makes 16 squares.

Maple Pecan Bars

3/4 cup melted butter, divided
3/4 cup brown sugar, divided
1 cup all-purpose flour
1 cup pure maple syrup
2 eggs, well beaten
2/3 cup chopped pecans
2 tablespoons all-purpose flour
1/2 teaspoon vanilla extract
1/4 teaspoon salt

In a bowl, combine ½ cup butter, ¼ cup brown sugar and flour. Press into 8x8x2-inch baking pan. Bake in a preheated 350-degree oven 10 minutes.

In a saucepan, combine remaining ¼ cup butter, remaining ½ cup brown sugar and maple syrup. Cook over low heat 5 minutes, or until sugar is dissolved. Let cool, then add eggs. Mix well. Stir in pecans, flour, vanilla and salt. Pour over baked crust. Bake in a 400-degree oven 5 minutes. Reduce oven temperature to 350 degrees; bake 30 minutes.

Makes 16 squares.

Wines & Beverages

Peach Wine Warmer

4 cups peach wine
4 whole allspice
4 whole cloves
4 cinnamon sticks
Honey

Pour 1 cup peach wine into each of 4 microwave-safe glass mugs. Add 1 whole allspice, 1 whole clove, and 1 cinnamon stick to each mug. Microwave on HIGH (100% power) 1 minute, or until warm. Do not boil. Add honey to taste and stir with cinnamon stick.
Makes 4 servings.

Left: Peach Wine Warmer

Raspberry Champagne Punch

1 can (6 ounces) frozen raspberry fruit juice cocktail, thawed
1/4 cup raspberry liqueur, optional
1 bottle (750 milliliter) champagne, chilled
Fresh or frozen whole raspberries

In a small punch bowl, combine fruit juice cocktail and liqueur. Slowly stir in champagne. Garnish with whole raspberries. Serve immediately.
Makes 10 servings.

White Wine Cooler

Ice cubes (about 30)
2 cups dry white wine
1 1/2 cups white grape juice
1 1/2 cups ginger ale
12 melon balls
6 orange slices

Fill a large pitcher half full of ice cubes. Add wine, grape juice and ginger ale. Mix well. Stir in melon balls and orange slices. Serve immediately.
Makes 6 servings.

Note: To make Pink Wine Cooler, substitute apple-cherry juice or a cherry juice blend for the white grape juice.

Sparkling Cherry Punch

4 cups apple-cherry juice or other cherry juice blend, chilled
1 quart ginger ale, chilled
Ice Ring (recipe follows) or ice cubes

Just before serving, combine juice and ginger ale in a large punch bowl. Add ice ring or ice cubes.
Makes 18 to 20 servings.

To make Ice Ring: Place a ring mold in freezer to chill well. Rinse inside of mold with cold water; return to freezer until thin coating of ice forms. Cover the bottom of the mold in a decorative pattern with drained mandarin orange sections and red maraschino cherries. Gently pour in enough water to just cover fruit. Freeze until firm. Gently pour in more water to fill mold completely. Freeze overnight, or until firm.

Spiced Apple Cider

1 teaspoon whole cloves
1 teaspoon whole allspice
1 (3-inch) stick cinnamon
1/2 cup firmly packed light
    brown sugar
2 quarts apple cider

Break up cloves, allspice and cinnamon using a rolling pin or meat hammer; put in a cheesecloth bag.

In a large saucepot, combine sugar and cider. Add cheesecloth bag of spices. Bring mixture to a boil over high heat. Reduce heat; simmer 20 minutes. Remove cheesecloth bag. Serve hot or cold.

Makes 20 servings.

Raspberry Yogurt Shake

1 cup fresh or frozen
    unsweetened raspberries
1 1/2 cups milk
1 cup frozen raspberry yogurt
    or raspberry sherbet
2 tablespoons honey

If using fresh raspberries, rinse them and drain well. If using frozen raspberries, thaw them before using.

In a blender container, combine raspberries, milk, yogurt and honey. Cover and blend on high speed until smooth. Serve immediately in tall, chilled glasses.

Makes 4 to 6 servings.

Maple Milk Shake

2 cups cold milk
1 pint vanilla ice cream, softened
1/2 cup maple syrup

In a blender container, combine milk, ice cream and maple syrup. Cover; blend until smooth and frothy. Serve immediately in tall, chilled glasses.

Makes 4 to 6 servings.

INDEX

Apple Dipper, 26
Apple Dumplings with Dried Cherries, 80
Apple Stuffed Celery, 26
Apples, 7
    Apple Dumpling with Dried Cherries, 80
    Carrot-Apple Salad, 38
    Great Lakes Green Salad, 35
    Sparkling Cherry Punch, 91
    Spiced Apple Cider, 92
    Traverse Bay Cherry-Nut Cake, 83
Asparagus Pasta Salad, 35
Asparagus, 7
    Asparagus Pasta Salad, 35
    Cream of Asparagus Soup, 33
    Marinated Asparagus, 76
Baked Brie with Strawberries, 25
Baked Celery, 75
Baked Ham with Sugared Plums, 60
Beans, 7
    Michigan Senate Bean Soup, 32
    Party Chili, 56
    Picnic Bean Salad, 37
Beef, 8
    Party Chili, 56
    Peppered Beef Kabobs, 55
    Poached Beef Tenderloin, 55
    Tailgate Roll-ups, 47
Blueberries, 8
    Blueberry Honey Sauce, 82
    Blueberry Muffins, 52
    Blueberry Sauced Veal Medallions, 58
    Maple Fresh Fruit Cup, 82
    Snowcap Blueberry Ice Cream Pie, 82
Blueberry Honey Sauce, 82
Blueberry Muffins, 52
Blueberry Sauced Veal Medallions, 58
Broccoli Quiche, 43
Broiled Tomatoes with Chevre, 76

Burgundy Lamb Chops, 62
Buttered Plum Waffles, 42
Carrots, 8
    Asparagus Pasta Salad, 35
    Carrot-Apple Salad, 38
    Honey Glazed Carrots, 78
Celery, 8
    Apple Stuffed Celery, 26
    Baked Celery, 75
    Hot Chicken and Celery Salad, 68
Cheddar Chive Crisps, 28
Cheddar Pine Cone, 27
Cheese Bread Bowls, 51
Cheese, 9
    Baked Brie with Strawberries, 25
    Broccoli Quiche, 43
    Cheddar Chive Crisps, 28
    Cheddar Pine Cone, 27
    Cheese Bread Bowls, 51
    Festive Oven Omelet, 42
    Grilled Cheddar Loaf, 50
Cheesecake Squares, 88
Cherries Jubilee, 84
Cherries, 8
    Apple Dumpling with Dried Cherries, 80
    Cherries Jubilee, 84
    Chocolate Cherry Cheesecake, 84
    Great Lakes Green Salad, 35
    Maple Fresh Fruit Cup, 86
    Sparkling Cherry Punch, 91
    Traverse Bay Cherry-Nut Cake, 83
    Turkey with Cherry Wine Sauce, 65
Chocolate Cherry Cheesecake, 84
Colorful Cabbage Salad, 38
Confetti Peppers, 78
Corn and Noodle Casserole, 77
Corn, 9
    Confetti Peppers, 78

Corn and Noodle Casserole, 77
Hot Peppery Corn-on-the-Cob, 77
Cream Cheese Frosting, 83
Cream Cheese, 9
    Cheesecake Squares, 88
    Chocolate Cherry Cheesecake, 84
    Cream Cheese Frosting, 83
    Green Onion Dip, 25
    Hot Florentine Dip, 27
    Raspberry Cream Cheese Torte, 86
    Superior Whitefish Pate, 24
Cream of Asparagus Soup, 33
Cucumber Soup, 33
Dried Cherry Vinaigrette, 35
Eggs, 11
    Broccoli Quiche, 43
    Festive Oven Omelet, 42
    Omelet in a Bread Round, 48
Festive Oven Omelet , 42
Fish Fillets with Garden Vegetables, 69
Fish, 12
    Fish Fillets with Garden Vegetables, 69
    Planked Whitefish, 70
    Superior Whitefish Pate, 24
Flowering Garden Salad, 37
Fresh Onion Soup, 32
Goat Cheese (Chevre), 9
    Broiled Tomatoes with Chevre, 76
    Great Lakes Green Salad, 35
    Stuffed Lamb with Honey Glaze, 63
Grapes, 9
    Maple Fresh Fruit Cup, 86
Great Lakes Green Salad, 35
Green Onion Dip, 25
Grilled Cheddar Loaf, 50
Grilled Chicken with Peach Salsa, 67
Grilled Stuffed Potato, 73
Herb Biscuits, 49

93

Herb Butter, 49
Herbed New Potatoes, 74
Herbs, 10
    Herb Biscuits, 49
    Herb Butter, 49
    Herbed New Potatoes, 74
    Pasta and Pesto, 36
Honey Glazed Carrots, 78
Honey, 10
    Blueberry Honey Sauce, 82
    Honey Glazed Carrots, 78
    Stuffed Lamb with Honey Glaze, 63
Hot Chicken and Celery Salad. 68
Hot Florentine Dip, 27
Hot Peppery Corn-on-the-Cob, 77
Ice Cream, 9
    Cherries Jubilee, 84
    Maple Milk Shake, 92
    Snowcap Blueberry Ice Cream Pie, 82
Lamb, 10
    Burgundy Lamb Chops, 62
    Roast Lamb with Mint Sauce, 64
    Stuffed Lamb with Honey Glaze, 63
Maple Barbecued Spareribs, 62
Maple Fresh Fruit Cup, 86
Maple Milk Shake, 92
Maple Pecan Bars, 88
Maple Syrup, 10
    Maple Barbecued Spareribs, 62
    Maple Fresh Fruit Cup, 86
    Maple Milk Shake, 92
    Maple Pecan Bars, 88
    Strawberry French Toast, 43
Marinated Asparagus, 76
Michigan Senate Bean Soup, 32
Mint Sauce, 64
Mushroom Stuffed Veal Breast, 59
Omelet in a Bread Round, 48
Onions, 10
    Broccoli Quiche, 43
    Fresh Onion Soup, 32

Green Onion Dip, 25
Grilled Cheddar Loaf, 50
Three Onion Tart, 40
Orchard Streusel Cake, 85
Party Chili, 56
Pasta and Pesto, 36
Peach Brunch Cake, 44
Peach Wine Warmer, 90
Peaches, 11
    Grilled Chicken with Peach Salsa, 67
    Maple Fresh Fruit Cup, 86
    Peach Brunch Cake, 44
    Peach Wine Warmer, 90
Pepper Beef Kabobs, 55
Picnic Bean Salad, 37
Planked Whitefish, 70
Plums, 11
    Baked Ham with Sugared Plums, 60
    Buttered Plum Waffles, 42
    Orchard Streusel Cake, 85
    Spiced Plum Bread, 52
Poached Beef Tenderloin, 55
Pork Medallions with Rosemary
    and Mushrooms, 60
Pork, 11
    Baked Ham with Sugared Plums, 60
    Hot Florentine Dip, 27
    Maple Barbecued Spareribs, 62
    Michigan Senate Bean Soup, 32
    Omelet in a Bread Round, 48
    Pork Medallions with Rosemary
        and Mushrooms, 60
Potatoes, 11
    Grilled Stuffed Potato. 73
    Herbed New Potatoes, 74
    Omelet in a Bread Round, 48
    Planked Whitefish, 70
    Potato Wedges, 73
Poultry, 11
    Grilled Chicken with Peach Salsa, 67
    Hot Chicken and Celery Salad, 68

Turkey with Cherry Wine Sauce, 65
Victory Pass Pate, 28
Pumpkin Soup, 30
Raspberry Champagne Punch, 91
Raspberry Cream Cheese Torte, 86
Raspberry Yogurt Shake, 92
Roast Lamb with Mint Sauce, 64
Seasoned Crumb Topping, 75
Snowcap Blueberry Ice Cream Pie, 82
Sparkling Cherry Punch, 91
Spiced Apple Cider, 92
Spiced Plum Bread, 52
Strawberries, 7
    Baked Brie with Strawberries, 25
    Maple Fresh Fruit Cup, 86
    Strawberry French Toast with Maple Surup, 43
Stuffed Lamb with Honey Glaze, 63
Sugar Beets, 12
Superior Whitefish Pate, 24
Tailgate Roll-ups, 47
Three Onion Tart, 40
Traverse Bay Cherry-Nut Cake, 83
Turkey with Cherry Wine Sauce, 65
Veal, 12
    Blueberry Sauced Veal Medallions, 58
    Mushroom Stuffed Veal Breast, 59
    Veal Mushroom Swiss Steak, 57
Victory Pass Pate, 28
Wine, 9
    Apple Dumplings with Dried Cherries, 80
    Burgundy Lamb Chops, 62
    Peach Wine Warmer, 90
    Poached Beef Tenderloin, 55
    Raspberry Champagne Punch, 91
    Turkey with Cherry Wine Sauce, 65
    Veal Mushroom Swiss Steak, 57
    Victory Pass Pate, 28
    White Wine Cooler, 91
Yogurt, 9
    Raspberry Yogurt Shake, 92
Zucchini Pockets, 47

Acknowledgments

To the Michigan Department of Agriculture and the commodity organizations for the grant to write this book and their ideas, enthusiasm and cooperation.

To the Michigan Veal Committee for their support, encouragement and partnership in producing and marketing this book.

To my husband, Pat, and daughters, Sara and Kristin, for their support, patience and willingness to sample the many recipes.

To Jane Baker of the Cherry Marketing Institute for her guidance and expertise in writing and editing.

To my mother, Carroll Whitehead, for her help in researching and testing recipes and for a lifetime of great meals.

To Michele Palmini and Tim Schroeder for their excellent work and for always going the extra mile to make each photograph "pretty great."

To my friends in retailing at Seasons, Pier I, Hudsons, and Jacobson's for letting me use their beautiful dishes and accessories.

To Nancy Parker for her diligence and commitment to produce a well designed cookbook with real flair.

To the restauranteurs of Michigan for their good food and ideas especially Tapawingo of Ellsworth, Schuler's of Marshall and Evergreen Grill of East Lansing.

About The Author

Gayle Main is a home economist, teacher and executive director of the Michigan Veal Committee. She is a graduate of Michigan State University and has been active in the food industry for many years as a writer, consultant, lecturer and food stylist. She lives in Okemos, Michigan with her husband, Pat, and daughters, Sara and Kristin.

Good Things Growing in Michigan

Great Lakes Sugar Beet Growers Association
Michigan Allied Poultry Industries
Michigan Apple Committee
Michigan Asparagus Advisory Board
Michigan Bean Commission
Michigan Beef Industry Commission
Michigan Beekeepers Association
Michigan Blueberry Growers Association
Michigan Celery Promotion Cooperative
Michigan Cherry Committee
Michigan Corn Growers Association
Michigan Dairy Goat Industry
Michigan Fish Producers Association
Michigan Fresh Market Carrot Committee
Michigan Grape and Wine Industry Council
Michigan Herb Business Association
Michigan Maple Syrup Producers Association
Michigan Onion Committee
Michigan Peach Sponsors
Michigan Plum Advisory Board
Michigan Pork Producers Association
Michigan Potato Industry Commission
Michigan Sheep Breeders Association
Michigan Veal Committee
United Dairy Industry of Michigan

Michigan Department of Agriculture